W9-CDY-351

The Practical Life of Faith

A Study of Hebrews 11–13

Bible Study Guide

From the Bible-teaching ministry of

Charles R. Swindoll

Insight for Living

Charles R. Swindoll is a graduate of Dallas Theological Seminary and has served in pastorates in Texas, Massachusetts, and California since 1963. He has served as senior pastor of the First Evangelical Free Church of Fullerton, California, since 1971. Chuck's radio program, "Insight for Living," began in 1979. In addition to his church and radio ministries, Chuck enjoys writing. He has authored numerous books and booklets on a variety of subjects.

Based on the outlines and transcripts of Chuck's sermons, the study guide text is coauthored by Ken Gire, a graduate of Texas Christian University and Dallas Theological Seminary. The Living Insights are written by Bill Butterworth, a graduate of Florida Bible College, Dallas Theological Seminary, and Florida Atlantic University.

Editor in Chief:
Cynthia Swindoll

Coauthor of Text:
Ken Gire

Author of Living Insights:
Bill Butterworth

Assistant Editor:
Glenda Schlahta

Copy Manager:
Jac La Tour

Copyediting Supervisor:
Marty Anderson

Copy Editor:
Wendy Peterson

Director, Communications Division:
Carla Beck

Project Manager:
Alene Cooper

Art Director:
Steven Mitchell

Designer:
Diana Vasquez

Production Artists:
Gary Lett and Diana Vasquez

Typographer:
Bob Haskins

Print Production Manager:
Deedee Snyder

Unless otherwise identified, all Scripture references are from the New American Standard Bible, © The Lockman Foundation 1960, 1962, 1963, 1968, 1971, 1972, 1973, 1975, 1977. Used by permission.

© 1989 Charles R. Swindoll. All rights reserved.

Previous guide:
© 1983 Charles R. Swindoll. All rights reserved.

Outlines and transcripts:
© 1982, 1983 Charles R. Swindoll. All rights reserved.

An effort has been made to locate sources and obtain permission where necessary for the quotations used in this book. In the event of any unintentional omission, a modification will gladly be incorporated in future printings.

Notice

No portion of this publication may be translated into any language or reproduced in any form, except for brief quotations in reviews, without prior written permission of the publisher, Insight for Living, Post Office Box 4444, Fullerton, California 92634.

ISBN 0-8499-8411-4
Printed in the United States of America.

COVER PAINTING: Ford Madox Brown's *Christ Washing Peter's Feet,* from Tate/ Art Resource, New York.

CONTENTS

1	How to Cure the Shrinks	1
2	Common Men of Uncommon Faith	9
3	A Faith Worth Duplicating	16
4	The Ultimate Test	23
5	Faith Served Family Style	30
6	Moses' Faith, Moses' Choices . . . and Me	37
7	By Faith, Miracles!	43
8	Triumphs and Tragedies of the Faithful	51
9	Arena Lifestyle	58
10	Flip Side of Love	64
11	Watch Out for Worldliness!	72
12	Our Awesome, Consuming God	79
13	Brothers, Strangers, and Prisoners	85
14	Commitment and Contentment (Part One)	92
15	Commitment and Contentment (Part Two)	98
16	My Responsibility to God-Appointed Leaders	104
17	Changeless Truths in a Shiftless World	112
18	Daring the Risk of Reach	120
19	Equipped to Do His Will	129
20	An Urgent Farewell	137
	Books for Probing Further	148
	Note Pages	150
	Ordering Information/Order Forms	155

INTRODUCTION

Having established the superiority of Christ in the first ten chapters, the writer to the Hebrews now shifts his emphasis to the most logical response—faith. Someone as preeminent as Christ deserves our wholehearted trust.

What great chapters these are! Not only are we able to meet the truly great men and women of faith, we are encouraged to follow their example by walking today as they walked then. With penetrating courage these concluding chapters challenge us to put feet to our belief . . . to become thoroughly Christian in lifestyle and response, with friend and stranger alike.

As we wrap up our study of this magnificent letter, won't you join me in expressing to God grateful thanks for including Hebrews in the Bible. Just think of the things we would have missed without it. May our life of faith reflect how much we respect and trust our preeminent Lord Jesus Christ.

Chuck Swindoll

Putting Truth into Action

Knowledge apart from application falls short of God's desire for His children. He wants us to apply what we learn so that we will change and grow. This study guide was prepared with these goals in mind. As you go through the following pages, we hope your desire to discover biblical truth will grow as your understanding of God's Word increases, and that you will be encouraged to apply what you've learned.

To assist you in your study, we've included a section called **Living Insights** at the end of each lesson. These exercises will challenge you to study further and to think of specific ways to put your discoveries into action.

There are many ways to use this guide—in personal devotions, group studies, discussions with friends and family, and Sunday school classes. And, of course, it's an ideal study aid when you're listening to its corresponding "Insight for Living" radio series.

To benefit most from this study guide, we would encourage you to consider it a spiritual journal. That's why we've included space in the **Living Insights** for recording your thoughts and discoveries. We hope you'll return to those sections often for review and encouragement as you continue to grow in your walk with Christ.

Ken Gire
Coauthor of Text

Bill Butterworth
Author of Living Insights

The Practical Life of Faith

A Study of Hebrews 11–13

Chapter 1

How to Cure the Shrinks

Hebrews 10:32–11:6

Nobody likes the waiting room of a doctor's office.

The scent of antiseptic smells more like impending danger than the aroma of health. The outdated magazines are dog-eared from previous patients' attentionless, nervous leafing. And from a distant room come the muffled shrieks of a child in pain. You draw your breath and steady your hand, trying to appear calm and adult about this routine physical checkup.

But you're not. Truth of the matter is, you're as scared as a school kid in for a booster shot. You fidget in your chair. Your eyes dart skittishly over the room as you wait for the nurse to massacre your last name. Your blood pressure is up—you can feel the flush in your face. When your name is called, you reluctantly follow a white polyester jacket into the examining room to endure the rituals of modern medicine. There's the humiliation of the disposable gown. The gag of the wooden tongue depressor. The stainless steel intimidation of sterile instruments lying in wait. The shine of the miner's lamp rudely intruding into your ears, nose, and throat. And the flutter of goosebumps over skin made to suffer the refrigerator-cold stethoscope.

Then there are the questions that always seem to be asked when you're holding your breath or when you've got something up your nose or in your mouth. And all of a sudden you feel like a four-year-old, fumbling around with one-syllable words and elementary school comparisons to describe how you feel.

It's no wonder nobody looks forward to the doctor's office. It's no wonder we shrink back from the battery of tests we're subjected to there—even though the results are for our benefit.

Like our family doctor, God periodically calls us in for an office visit and subjects our faith to a rigorous regimen of uncomfortable tests. Most often, we respond to those tests the way we respond to a doctor's appointment. We develop a case of the shrinks.

To cure this phobia, James gives us some valuable advice.

> When all kinds of trials and temptations crowd into your lives, my brothers, don't resent them as intruders, but welcome them as friends! Realise that they come to test your faith and to produce in you the quality of endurance. But let the process go on until that endurance is fully developed, and you will find you have become men of mature character with the right sort of independence. (James 1:2–4)[1]

A Brief Analysis of Shrinking

At the beginning of a test, our faith is challenged. At the end, it is rewarded. It's during the middle of the test that real stress comes—but that's precisely where our faith is strengthened.

It is in the disillusioning wilderness of waiting that the roots of our faith are driven deeper. This in-between time when we are in greatest danger of shrinking back is the subject of today's passage. The scorching sands of the wilderness weren't foreign to the bare feet of the first-century Christians, as the writer of Hebrews indicates in 10:32.

> But remember the former days, when, after being enlightened, you endured a great conflict of sufferings.

The term rendered *conflict* is the word *athlēsis,* from which we get our word *athletics.* The picture is of a grueling athletic contest like those exhibited in the Colosseum. The writer breaks these conflicts into four groups.

The Test of Others' Tongues

> Partly, by being made a public spectacle through reproaches and tribulations, and partly by becoming sharers with those who were so treated. (v. 33)

1. J. B. Phillips, The New Testament in Modern English (London, England: Geoffrey Bles, 1960).

The term *spectacle* comes from the Greek word that means "theater." The Christians were being placed on stage, so to speak, and made a theatrical spectacle through "reproaches." The Greek term brings to mind "defamation"—being made the object of disgrace through verbal abuse.

The Test of Others' Actions

The term *tribulations* in verse 33 refers to overt affliction. "Mistreatment" would be a good translation.

The Test of Indirect Suffering

To undergo *direct* suffering when someone is making your life miserable is *certainly* a test. But it is often a more stringent test to suffer *vicariously* as we see someone we love being squeezed by the winepress of persecution. That's what verse 33 refers to by "becoming sharers with those who were so treated."

The Test of Losing Valuable Things

The fourth category of suffering the writer alludes to is found in verse 34.

> For you showed sympathy to the prisoners, and accepted joyfully the seizure of your property, knowing that you have for yourselves a better possession and an abiding one.

The Hebrew Christians endured the seizure of their property, but suffering also results from losing things more valuable than property. Like our loved ones. Our reputation. Our health. Our freedom.

The sufferings of those early Christians were similar to the sufferings of prisoners in the Russian *gulags* (labor camps) under Stalin's regime. There the interrogators would break them down with verbal abuse, psychological intimidation, and finally the cruelest forms of physical abuse. Aleksandr Solzhenitsyn chronicles this kind of suffering in *The Gulag Archipelago.* In it he tells how he managed to endure the cruel fist of his captors. His advice will help us all survive the searing heat of the most relentless of trials.

> How can you stand your ground when you are weak and sensitive to pain, when people you love are still alive, when you are unprepared?
>
> What do you need to make you stronger than the interrogator and the whole trap?
>
> From the moment you go to prison you must put your cozy past firmly behind you. At the very threshold,

> you must say to yourself: "My life is over, a little early to be sure, but there's nothing to be done about it. I shall never return to freedom. I am condemned to die—now or a little later. But later on, in truth, it will be even harder, and so the sooner the better. I no longer have any property whatsoever. For me those I love have died, and for them I have died. From today on, my body is useless and alien to me. Only my spirit and my conscience remain precious and important to me."
>
> Confronted by such a prisoner, the interrogation will tremble.
>
> Only the man who has renounced everything can win that victory.[2]

Victory in the spiritual realm is reserved for those who have loosened their hold on everything but Christ. Of all who shoulder the burden of suffering, they are the ones with the greatest chance of bearing up under its crippling load.

What should give us the strength to endure the sweltering journey is the promise of a better and abiding possession.

> Therefore, do not throw away your confidence, which has a great reward. For you have need of endurance, so that when you have done the will of God, you may receive what was promised.
>
> For yet in a very little while,
> He who is coming will come, and will
> not delay.
> But My righteous one shall live by faith;
> And if he shrinks back, My soul has no
> pleasure in him.
>
> But we are not of those who shrink back to destruction, but of those who have faith to the preserving of the soul. (vv. 35–39)

The word *endurance* in verse 36 is from the Greek verb *hupomeno.* It means "abiding under, staying with it, not giving up or giving in." Endurance is what gives us a second wind and a will to go on. And that comes through faith. The alternative to faith? To "shrink back." The word is *hupostellō.* It is the opposite of *hupomeno.* It means "to retreat, to find a way out."

2. Aleksandr I. Solzhenitsyn, *The Gulag Archipelago: 1918–1956,* trans. Thomas P. Whitney (New York, N.Y.: Harper and Row, Publishers, 1974), vols. 1 and 2, p. 130.

Faith: The Alternative to Shrinking

Since living by faith is the way the righteous are to live if they want to please God, a definition of faith is in order. That definition is the hinge which swings us into chapter 11.

> Now faith is the assurance of things hoped for, the conviction of things not seen. For by it the men of old gained approval. By faith we understand that the worlds were prepared by the word of God, so that what is seen was not made out of things which are visible. By faith Abel offered to God a better sacrifice than Cain, through which he obtained the testimony that he was righteous, God testifying about his gifts, and through faith, though he is dead, he still speaks. By faith Enoch was taken up so that he should not see death; and he was not found because God took him up; for he obtained the witness that before his being taken up he was pleasing to God. And without faith it is impossible to please Him, for he who comes to God must believe that He is, and that He is a rewarder of those who seek Him. (vv. 1–6)

Faith will never grow strong apart from the stress of enduring strenuous trials. Like a muscle it must be exercised or it will atrophy. Chapter 11 is a gymnasium of God's finest specimens of faith. There we see spiritual muscles stretched to the limit. But with each exhausting workout, faith grew stronger. A careful look at verses 1–6 reveals five important truths that made their faith vital.

First: *Faith involves confidence and conviction* (v. 1). The word *assurance* in verse 1 comes from the term meaning "to stand under." It often refers to a foundation that undergirds a building or to a title that documents ownership of property. *Conviction* means "proof," like courtroom exhibits of evidence. Without this inner confidence and conviction, it is impossible to comprehend the unseen world of spiritual reality.

Second: *Faith always relates to the future* (v. 1). Faith is the assurance of things *hoped for*—the cement we mix into hope to harden it. Without faith, our hope is little more than a slush of wishful thinking.

Third: *Faith has as its object "things not seen"* (v. 1). When we focus on the unseen, we develop an incredible ability to envision what God will one day make visible.

Fourth: *Faith is basic to pleasing God* (vv. 2, 6). By it we gain the approval of God, as Enoch did (v. 5). There is no substitute to faith when it comes to pleasing God. No amount of good works, no amount of sacrifice, no amount of religious activity can make up for what is lacking in our faith.

Fifth: *Faith means focusing fully on God* (v. 6). To seek God in a manner that would evoke His reward means centering our attention and our affection solely on Him. When we do, we gain a greater glimpse of His power and presence. And our faith grows in proportion to the greatness of that glimpse.

Solving the Shrinking Syndrome

Do you find yourself shrinking back from the tests God has authorized for your life? If so, the following three-part prescription may help. First, *ask yourself the questions:* Why is faith such a constant struggle for me? Do I have some unresolved conflicts, some lingering bitterness that I've not released to the Lord? Second, *do yourself a favor:* Bite off life in daily chunks. Live life a day at a time. Focus on today and don't be anxious about tomorrow, for as the Lord said: "Tomorrow will care for itself" (Matt. 6:34). Third, *find yourself a friend:* Look for someone who can help support you when your knees start buckling, someone who can shoulder the load when it gets too heavy, someone who can cry with you when the pain is simply too much to bear alone (Eccles. 4:9–12, Gal. 6:2, Rom. 12:15).

Finally, a closing thought from Madeleine L'Engle's excellent book, *Walking on Water*: "Faith is what makes life bearable, with all its tragedies and ambiguities and sudden, startling joys."[3]

Living Insights — STUDY ONE

This series will be based on the eleventh, twelfth, and thirteenth chapters of Hebrews. Let's use today's time to acquaint ourselves with this great section of God's Word.

- Begin reading these chapters. As you read, jot down any questions or observations that may come to you along the way. This exercise will help you fine-tune your thinking for the messages ahead.

3. Madeleine L'Engle, *Walking on Water: Reflections on Faith and Art* (Wheaton, Ill.: Harold Shaw Publishers, 1980), p. 22.

Hebrews 11–13: Questions and Observations

Living Insights STUDY TWO

Are you suffering from the "shrinking" syndrome? Our study closed with a prescription that we can begin applying by asking ourselves some questions, doing ourselves a favor, and finding ourselves a friend.

- Is faith a constant struggle for you? Do you have some unresolved conflicts, some lingering bitterness that you've not released to the Lord? If so, try to pinpoint the problem, using the space provided.

____

____

____

____

____

- What can you do to help focus more on today's priorities rather than tomorrow's problems?

____

____

____

____

- Read Matthew 6 and Luke 10:38–42 and see if that helps simplify the task of living.
- Think of your three closest friends. With a copy of *The Friendship Factor* by Alan Loy McGinnis in hand, evaluate those three relationships in light of its advice.

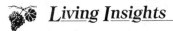

Chapter 2

Common Men of Uncommon Faith

Hebrews 11:1–7

A Christian who lives by faith is something of an enigma. In his book *The Root of the Righteous,* A. W. Tozer makes eloquent note of this fact.

> A real Christian is an odd number anyway. He feels supreme love for One whom he has never seen, talks familiarly every day to Someone he cannot see, expects to go to heaven on the virtue of Another, empties himself in order to be full, admits he is wrong so he can be declared right, goes down in order to get up, is strongest when he is weakest, richest when he is poorest, and happiest when he feels worst. He dies so he can live, forsakes in order to have, gives away so he can keep, sees the invisible, hears the inaudible, and knows that which passeth knowledge.[1]

Functioning somewhat like a *Reader's Digest* condensed version of the Old Testament, Hebrews 11 recounts biblical history through common men and women who demonstrated uncommon faith—faith that perplexed the people around them but that pleased the God above them.

A Brief, Simple Analysis of Faith

Before the writer documents the journey of the faithful, he defines the faith which made that journey possible in the first place.

> Now faith is the assurance of things hoped for, the conviction of things not seen. (Heb. 11:1)

Faith is not a blind leap in the dark; it's more like the sure step of a trusting child toward the loving arms of its mother. Faith is confidence in God, that He is there, that He cares, that He is faithful, that He intervenes . . . and that He embraces us when we throw ourselves into His arms.

1. A. W. Tozer, *The Root of the Righteous* (Camp Hill, Pa.: Christian Publications, 1986), p. 156.

Have you ever noticed how faith comes so easily to children and yet with so much difficulty to adults? When Jesus healed the lame and the blind in the temple, for example, children were the ones shouting His praises; the adults were the ones who sat back skeptically and became indignant (Matt. 21:14–15).[2]

The simplicity of childlike faith is described for us in Hebrews 11:6.

> And without faith it is impossible to please Him, for He who comes to God must believe that He is, and that He is a rewarder of those who seek Him.

The steps to pleasing God are as simple as the baby steps of a toddler. First, we come to God. Second, we believe He's there. Third, we count on Him to keep His Word.

Dag Hammarskjöld, in his journal, describes the believer of old who exhibited that kind of childlike faith.

> He broke fresh ground—because, and only because, he had the courage to go ahead without asking whether others were following or even understood. He had no need for the divided responsibility in which others seek to be safe from ridicule, because he had been granted a faith which required no confirmation.[3]

That is the type of faith that pleases God. But there are risks to that type of faith, just as there are risks when children toddle to their parents. They can fall flat on their faces. They can bruise a leg. They can bend back a finger as they try to brace their fall.

However, the risks need to be weighed against the rewards. Those rewards are found in the arms of the loving parent—not in the padded security of the playpen. And those risks are, in reality, negligible because of the trustworthy character of God. Consequently, we can step out, knowing that He will be there to embrace us, to catch us if we start to fall, and to soothe our hurts with a compassionate kiss.

Three Plain, Common Examples of Faith

Those who stepped out in Hebrews 11 weren't fully grown and mature in faith. They were uncoordinated toddlers, with tenuous

2. See also the contrast between the disciples and the children in Matthew 18:1–4.

3. Dag Hammarskjöld, *Markings*, trans. Leif Sjöberg and W. H. Auden (New York, N.Y.: Alfred A. Knopf, 1964), p. 110.

legs and mincing steps. They were weak, sinful, subject to depression and fear. They were, in a word, human—just like us (James 5:17).

Three of those people are the focus of today's study. One was merely a shepherd, one merely a preacher, and one merely a builder.

A Shepherd Named Abel

Hebrews 11:4 introduces us to our first man of faith.

> By faith Abel offered to God a better sacrifice than Cain, through which he obtained the testimony that he was righteous, God testifying about his gifts, and through faith, though he is dead, he still speaks.

Abel—a common man. With the mention of this name we go back in time to a primitive era when life was simple and serene. No smog. No clogged highways. No fighting for parking spaces.

Genesis 4 tells us that Abel kept sheep, while his brother Cain was a tiller of the soil (v. 2). Implied in the account is an important fact—that God had informed both brothers of the type of offering He expected. It was to be a blood sacrifice. Abel obeyed. Cain, however, chose to offer the work of his hands. Cain came to God by his own way; Abel came God's way. Abel's faith was evidenced in his offering; Cain's lack of faith was evidenced in his.

Undoubtedly Cain was sincere. But sincerity is no substitute for obedience.

It's human nature to want to come to God in our own way, on our own terms, with the offering of our own good works. But that is not God's way. God's way is through another offering—the shed blood of His only Son (Heb. 9:11–14). And when we come to God, it can be only through faith in Jesus; not through the work of our hands, no matter how hard or how long we've toiled or how plentiful the harvest.

A Preacher Named Enoch

Hebrews 11:5 encapsulates the life of an obscure believer named Enoch.

> By faith Enoch was taken up so that he should not see death; and he was not found because God took him up; for he obtained the witness that before his being taken up he was pleasing to God.

The biography of Enoch is, at best, sketchy. Besides this verse, we have only a couple of verses in Jude that remark on his public life (see vv. 14–15) and some verses in Genesis that collect a few fragments of his private life. Publicly, he proclaimed a message that his wicked generation resented and resisted. Privately, Enoch raised a son and walked with God.

> And Enoch lived sixty-five years, and became the father of Methuselah. Then Enoch walked with God three hundred years after he became the father of Methuselah, and he had other sons and daughters. So all the days of Enoch were three hundred and sixty-five years. And Enoch walked with God; and he was not, for God took him. (Gen. 5:21–24)

Perhaps it was the childlike faith Enoch saw in his son that prompted him to take the first steps in his walk with God. Perhaps it was the awesome responsibility of raising his son amidst the wickedness of his culture that turned him toward God. We don't know for sure. But we do know that his faith, which kept him in step with God and out of step with his wayward generation, pleased the Father. That faith not only put Enoch in Hebrews 11, it took him to heaven without having to experience death (Gen. 5:24).

A Builder Named Noah

As the writer of Hebrews thumbs through the book of Genesis, he comes to a well-worn, dog-eared page that tells the story of a man of uncommon faith—Noah. The writer distills entire chapters of this man's life into just one verse.

> By faith Noah, being warned by God about things not yet seen, in reverence prepared an ark for the salvation of his household, by which he condemned the world, and became an heir of the righteousness which is according to faith. (Heb. 11:7)

Talk about being out of step with your generation—Noah was definitely walking to the beat of a different drummer.[4] Think of how ludicrous the building project must have seemed in the eyes of his contemporaries. No rain had yet fallen on the earth. No large bodies of water existed within five hundred miles.[5] The boat was a thousand

4. Noah is described in Genesis as a righteous man, blameless in his generation, one who walked with God and who found favor in His eyes (6:8–9). His contemporaries, however, were wicked, with every intent of their thoughts and hearts continually focused on evil (v. 5).

5. An excellent resource about the flood is *The Genesis Flood* (Phillipsburg, N.J.: Presbyterian and Reformed, 1961) by John C. Whitcomb, Jr., and Henry M. Morris.

times too big for his family, being about twice the length of a football field, almost a football field in width, and four stories high (Gen. 6:15). And to make Noah an even greater laughingstock, it took over a hundred years to build.

Yet in spite of how outrageous the objective or seemingly maniacal the method, Noah obeyed the instructions of God (v. 22; 7:5, 9, 16). He acted in faith, believing God's word over the public opinion polls about his sanity.

Two Direct, Relevant Applications of Faith

Abel, Enoch, and Noah. All common men, but each with an uncommon faith.

By faith, Abel came God's way.

By faith, Enoch proclaimed God's word.

By faith, Noah fulfilled God's will.

But for the time being, let's leave their lives to historians and archeologists. How about your life? If faith were the topic of conversation in your neighborhood, would your name come up? If Hebrews 11 were to be updated in heaven, would your name be on the list?

Whether you're making an offering to God, speaking out on His behalf, or obeying His Word, God looks for one thing—faith. A faith that's willing to step out, no matter how weak its toddling steps. And a faith that seeks the arms of God rather than the embrace of the world.

Living Insights — STUDY ONE

Abel, Enoch, and Noah were common men who exhibited uncommon faith. By faith, Abel came God's way. By faith, Enoch proclaimed God's word. By faith, Noah fulfilled God's will. Take a minute to filter your life through theirs.

- Is your approach to God based on His way or is it according to yours? Are you coming to Him Cain's way—by your own works? Or are you coming to Him Abel's way—by faith? This can apply to salvation as well as your daily fellowship with Him.

- Since faith comes by hearing and hearing by the Word of God, your proclaiming the Word to another is an essential precursor to that person's salvation. Is there someone specific with whom God has burdened your heart to share the gospel? Think through the Bible passages you're familiar with and pray for wisdom to discern which would be the most appropriate to share with that person. What passage did the Holy Spirit put on your heart?

____

- Write down what God is revealing to you that would take a faith like Noah's to accomplish.

____

____

What steps are you taking to fulfill His will in this specific area of your life?

____

____

____

____

Living Insights STUDY TWO

The title of today's lesson teaches us an important truth: all the men and women in Hebrews 11 were common people. It was their faith that was uncommon. So, fellow commoner, there is room for us in Hebrews 11!

- We closed our study with two penetrating questions. Let's take time to answer them in detail.

    1. If faith were the topic of conversation in your neighborhood, would your name come up? Why or why not?

____

____

____

____

____

2. If Hebrews 11 were to be updated in heaven, would your name be on the list? Why or why not?

Chapter 3

A Faith Worth Duplicating

Hebrews 11:8–16

Exactly what is it that pleases God?

It seems that in the hard business of living life, this should be the bottom-line question for the believer.

Does doing the sensational please Him? Some enigmatic verses in Mark talk about believers being able to pick up serpents and drink deadly poison without being harmed (16:17–18). But does God expect us to demonstrate life-threatening feats of faith to please Him? Or is seeking such extraordinary displays more along the lines of Satan challenging Jesus to make a sensational statement of faith by jumping off the pinnacle of the temple (Matt. 4:5–6)? If you remember, that challenge was met with a rebuke (v. 7).

Do we please God by putting out a fleece as did Gideon (Judg. 6:36–40)? Or was that more an expression of doubt than of faith (see also vv. 11–18, 21, 36)?

Do we please God when we leap to conclusions drawn from mere coincidences? Or is that more like playing around with some sort of sanctified Ouija board, asking circumstances to guide us rather than God's Word and His Spirit?

What It Takes to Please God

If the sensational and the superstitious fall short of pleasing God, what is it, then, that does please Him? Hebrews 11:6 provides the answer.

> And without faith it is impossible to please Him, for he who comes to God must believe that He is, and that He is a rewarder of those who seek Him.

Pleasing God takes faith, and that includes three things. First, *coming to God.* Faith is an approach to God that is characterized by an attitude of total dependence. Second, *believing that He is there.* Faith involves an unswerving confidence in His presence, which we can't see, and in His concern, which we may not feel. Third, *trusting God to keep His Word.* Faith relies on His promise to reward such trust.

Faith involves risking, resting, and relying—things that Abel, Enoch, and Noah did (vv. 4–7), as we learned in our last lesson. In the verses that follow, the writer to the Hebrews introduces a married couple whose lives were characterized by faith—Abraham and Sarah. Twelve verses are reserved for them in Hebrews 11, more than anyone else eulogized in this immortal Hall of Faith.

Truly, as we shall see, theirs is a faith worth duplicating.

How Faith Was Expressed in Two Ancient Lives

The faith of Abraham and Sarah was neither sensational nor superstitious, but was sourced in the sure promise of God. Let's first examine Abraham's faith in verses 8–10; then we'll take a look at Sarah's.

> By faith Abraham, when he was called, obeyed by going out to a place which he was to receive for an inheritance; and he went out, not knowing where he was going. By faith he lived as an alien in the land of promise, as in a foreign land, dwelling in tents with Isaac and Jacob, fellow heirs of the same promise; for he was looking for the city which has foundations, whose architect and builder is God.

When Abraham was called, he responded obediently. His trust wasn't subjective but was grounded on the objective word of God. Notice how clear the calling is in Genesis 12:1.

> Now the Lord said to Abram,
> "Go forth from your country,
> And from your relatives
> And from your father's house,
> To the land which I will show you."

Abraham didn't see a billowy cloud formation that reminded him of God. He didn't hear a peal of thunder echoing in his ear or see lightning pointing the direction he should go. Quite the contrary. Abraham heard the very voice of God, and that voice was audible, objective, and specific.

That is where faith rests—in the word of God (Rom. 10:17).

Two remarkable phrases in Hebrews 11:8 communicate encyclopedias about Abraham's faith: "he went out" and "not knowing where he was going." The fact that he left his homeland at the drop of a few sentences from the lips of God was incredible. After all, he wasn't a young, upwardly mobile professional who could pull up tent stakes and relocate across country with just two weeks' notice. He was seventy-five years old, married, and had a lifetime of accumulated possessions (Gen. 12:5). On top of that, there wasn't a Desert Van Lines or even so much as a U-Haul to make his adventure in moving any smoother.

To complicate things, Abraham was given no road map of the journey. He didn't know where he was going or how long it would take. Can you imagine him trying to explain all this to his father-in-law, let alone the rest of his relatives? They must have thought a tent peg had popped loose in his mind.

You might think that once Abraham reached the Promised Land, he could settle in and put down roots. But such was not the case, as Hebrews 11:9 indicates.

> By faith he lived as an alien in the land of promise, as in a foreign land, dwelling in tents with Isaac and Jacob, fellow heirs of the same promise.

Abraham lived as a foreigner in a land where he had no rights of citizenship. Furthermore, he lived there with not so much as a square foot of land to his name (Acts 7:3–5).

You can't help but stand back and ask yourself, How could an intelligent man like Abraham make such rash and irresponsible decisions? How could he subject his wife to that type of life—without roots, without neighbors, without some source of security?

Hebrews 11:10 gives us a clue.

> For he was looking for the city which has foundations, whose architect and builder is God.

Abraham's focus wasn't on the sand and grit and heat of the journey, nor was it on the tent in which he lived. He saw beyond all that to something eternal. He envisioned not a literal city, bustling with highways and high rises, but a scene that transcended earth to that permanent, eternal home of the faithful (Heb. 12:18–19, 22–24).

But while Abraham had his eyes on distant horizons, what was going on in his wife's mind? Was Sarah frustrated, fuming about her husband's flighty and farfetched plans? Was she irritated, kicking and screaming as she packed her bags and mounted her camel for the long caravan ride through the desert? We have no record if she did. On the contrary, the cameos of her in Scripture underscore her submissive nature (1 Pet. 3:6) and her childlike faith:

> By *faith* even Sarah herself received ability to conceive, even beyond the proper time of life, since *she considered Him faithful who had promised;* therefore, also, there was born of one man, and him as good as dead at that, as many descendants as the stars of heaven in number, and innumerable as the sand which is by the seashore. (Heb. 11:11–12, emphasis added)

Sarah's initial reaction to the incredulous news of a son was a blurt of laughter, as she and her husband were both well beyond the childbearing years (Gen. 18:9–15). But as sure as God had spoken, Sarah did give birth to a son (21:1–2). Abraham was one hundred years old at the time Isaac was born; Sarah was ninety. The writer uses the same phrase to describe Sarah that he used to describe Abraham—*by faith.* The phrase reveals volumes about her life. Though initially she laughed at the revelation, she later came to embrace it with the warm reception of faith. And that faith put her in something far greater than the *Guinness Book of World Records;* it brought her to that eternal city of Hebrews 11:10.

Principles That Continue to This Day

The unique example of Abraham and Sarah can be confusing when you try to derive principles from their lives and apply them to today. However, verses 13–16 help. The first principle is *vision.*

> All these died in faith, without receiving the promises, but having seen them and having welcomed them from a distance, and having confessed that they were strangers and exiles on the earth. (v. 13)

Vision is the ability to hope beyond the restrictions of the present. Abraham and Sarah found hope beyond the limited horizons of this earth as they looked to God's promises waiting for them on the shimmering horizons of eternity. So enticing were those promises that nothing on earth could recapture their hearts. As far as they were concerned, everywhere they went they were foreigners; their real home was heaven.

By the way, how is your vision? Is it focused on the things of this earth and blurred toward heavenly things? Or are your eyes so fixed on heaven that everything else pales by comparison (see Phil. 3:17–21)?

The second principle is *pursuit.*

> For those who say such things make it clear that they are seeking a country of their own. (Heb. 11:14)

Abraham and Sarah were seeking a real homeland, a pursuit which is, in essence, a determination to cultivate an identity with God. What kind of pursuit have you embarked on? Is it trivial or eternal? Look up Matthew 6:25–33; it should help guide your course.

The third principle is *abandonment.*

> And indeed if they had been thinking of that country from which they went out, they would have had opportunity to return. (Heb. 11:15)

Abandonment is withdrawal. It is saying good-bye to something —forever. It's leaving without looking back. No physical blockade refused Abraham and Sarah the privilege of returning. No bridges were actually burned—at least physically. It was their attitude of abandonment, the bridges they had torched in their minds, that prevented their return.

As you step out in faith, are you timidly feeling around with your toes, testing the ground to make sure it will support your weight? Or are you burning bridges and blazing a pioneer's trail of faith?

The fourth principle is *desire.*

> But as it is, they desire a better country, that is a heavenly one. Therefore God is not ashamed to be called their God; for He has prepared a city for them. (v. 16)

The term *desire* means "to stretch out after" or "yearn after" something. It's a yearning after something more enticing than anything you've ever seen in *Better Homes and Gardens.* Something more endearing than all the Norman Rockwells put together. Something more enduring than blue-chip stock. It's a lifestyle, actually, of daily reaching out for the most God has to offer (Ps. 42:1–2a).

Why a Life of Faith Is So Rare

One question is left begging like a stray dog for a scrap of meat: If a life of faith is so great, why do so few people live it? An important reason is that most people would rather do anything than risk.

Taking risks means becoming vulnerable. And that may affect our finances, our friends, our future, our feelings, our occupation, where we live, and a host of other considerations. The human tendency is to want to be safe and secure, to hedge our bets, to insure ourselves against loss. Basically, we fail at faith because we fear to risk.

Another reason why a life of faith is so seldom found is because most who walk by faith do nothing to publicize it. They don't headline it in the news or rent the Goodyear blimp to advertise it. They model it quietly, like servants whose sole interest is to serve their master. Without ostentation. Without orchestration.

Are you willing to risk? Are you ready to be a model for the Hebrews 11 type of faith? If you're still teetering and need a little push to help you decide, Jim Elliot's words will galvanize you.

> "He is no fool who gives what he cannot keep to gain what he cannot lose."[1]

Living Insights STUDY ONE

Take a few minutes to examine another commentary on Abraham's life—Paul's, in Romans 4:18–22.

> In hope against hope he believed, in order that he might become a father of many nations, according to that which had been spoken, "So shall your descendants be." And without becoming weak in faith he contemplated his own body, now as good as dead since he was about a hundred years old, and the deadness of Sarah's womb; yet, with respect to the promise of God, he did not waver in unbelief, but grew strong in faith, giving glory to God, and being fully assured that what He had promised, He was able also to perform. Therefore also it was reckoned to him as righteousness.

With Abraham's example in mind, think about your faith. Is there some area of your life in which you're having trouble trusting God? Isolate that area.

Now try to isolate the reason why you're wavering.

1. Jim Elliot, as quoted by Elisabeth Elliot in *Shadow of the Almighty* (New York, N.Y.: Harper and Brothers, Publishers, 1958), p. 15.

Since faith comes by hearing and hearing by the Word of God (Rom. 10:17), it stands to reason that to grow strong in faith, we must sink our roots into His Word. In the space provided, list several verses that relate to the area in which you're having trouble trusting God. As you look them up, meditate on them, determine to take God at His word, and see if they don't strengthen your faith!

______________________ ______________________

______________________ ______________________

______________________ ______________________

Living Insights STUDY TWO

Abraham and Sarah are incredible models of faith and confidence in God. But the faith lifestyle isn't limited to biblical days; we can experience that lifestyle today!

- Let's take this little quiz. Circle the appropriate answer:

  Would you be characterized as a person of vision?

  No   Mostly No   Mostly Yes   Yes

  Are you pursuing eternal things?

  No   Mostly No   Mostly Yes   Yes

  Are you a person characterized by abandonment?

  No   Mostly No   Mostly Yes   Yes

  Do you desire, *yearn after,* the things of God?

  No   Mostly No   Mostly Yes   Yes

- Now, think up a strategy on how to boost one of your lower scores. Make the strategy simple, practical, and attainable.

  ____

  ____

  ____

  ____

  ____

Chapter 4

THE ULTIMATE TEST

Hebrews 11:17–19, Genesis 22

If you've ever been to a cardiologist, you probably know what a stress test is like. They hook you up to a monitor, then put you on a treadmill, turning up the speed until the monitor reveals the condition of your heart. And all the while, you're walking your dogs off trying to keep up with the treadmill.

After several sweaty minutes, the treadmill is turned off and the monitor completes its printed readout. Those results tell the cardiologist the true condition of your heart.

In a similar manner, God puts us all through stress tests at different times in our lives. He does this not to precipitate a heart attack but to give us a diagnosis concerning the condition of our faith.

There's something about seeing an actual printout of an EKG that keeps us from fooling ourselves about the condition of our hearts. And there's something about the results of God's tests that forces us to come to grips with the condition of our faith. We may be able to fake it in the pew or at prayer meetings, but God's strenuous testing shows our faith for what it is.

But these tests are not designed only to reveal the weakness of our faith; they are designed to strengthen it as well. That rigorous exercise on a sometimes tedious treadmill of tests can move us from a sedentary faith to an aerobic, active faith.

Test Levels: A General Appraisal

Second Corinthians 4:8–9 suggests that there are four basic levels of tests.

> We are afflicted in every way, but not crushed; perplexed, but not despairing; persecuted, but not forsaken; struck down, but not destroyed.

The most moderate level of testing is *affliction.* The original term suggests "pressure." This level includes tests that come from people, from deadlines, from delays, from irritating interruptions.

The second level is *being perplexed.* The term means "without a way" and suggests confusion, not knowing where to go or who to turn to when the speed on the treadmill is turned up and ordinary pressures intensify. This includes circumstances where we're subjected to unfair treatment by unfair people and we have difficulty making sense of it all and knowing what to do.

The third level is *persecution.* The term means "to run after, to pursue." These are the more extreme tests, when not only is the treadmill running on high speed but a pit bull is hot on your heels. Persecution can attack in a number of different areas: physical, emotional, financial, social, and spiritual.

The fourth level is *being struck down.* The term means "to be thrown down, shoved aside, rejected." This is the deepest level, the ultimate test. It could include the taking away or tearing down of that which is most precious and dear to your heart. Many times it involves disability or death. For Abraham, the ultimate test involved the fate of his beloved son.

Abraham's Ultimate Test

Scripture records Abraham's excruciating test in two separate places. The telescopic overview is recorded in Hebrews 11. The microscopic analysis is chronicled in Genesis 22. Let's look through both lenses to see what help this 3,800-year-old test offers for us today.

An Overview in Hebrews 11

The dramatic story is condensed in verses 17–19.

> By faith Abraham, when he was tested, offered up Isaac; and he who had received the promises was offering up his only begotten son; it was he to whom it was said, "In Isaac your descendants shall be called." He considered that God is able to raise men even from the dead; from which he also received him back as a type.

Imagine the shock Abraham must have felt when God told him to sacrifice Isaac. Put yourself in his shoes and try to make sense of the command. Imagine the disillusionment. How could a compassionate God impose such a cruel test? How could a God who is faithful to His promise now seemingly go back on that promise? How could a fair God take away that which He had given?

Shock and disillusionment are common reactions to a level-four test. Abraham's response, however, was one of unquestioning trust; he knew that God couldn't lie, and he knew that God wasn't capricious with His gifts. Therefore, raising Isaac from the dead was the logical conclusion of faith's reasoning.[1]

An Analysis in Genesis 22

We've gotten a look at the broad picture in Hebrews 11; now let's get a closer view of some of the story's details in Genesis 22.

> Now it came about after these things, that God tested[2] Abraham, and said to him, "Abraham!" And he said, "Here I am." And He said, "Take now your son, your only son, whom you love, Isaac, and go to the land of Moriah; and offer him there as a burnt offering[3] on one of the mountains of which I will tell you." (vv. 1–2)

Look again at the way God refers to Isaac: "your son, your only son, whom you love." Don't think for a moment that God doesn't know about those things in our lives that we come close to idolizing. He can name every idol of our lives, every precious possession, every relationship that competes for His love. He knew about that apple of Abraham's eye, and He knew it was time to put his priorities in perspective.

Abraham's response to this test is nothing short of remarkable.

> So Abraham rose early in the morning and saddled his donkey, and took two of his young men with him and Isaac his son; and he split wood for the burnt offering, and arose and went to the place of which God had told him. On the third day Abraham raised his eyes and saw the place from a distance. And Abraham said to his young men, "Stay here with the donkey, and I and the lad will go yonder; and we will worship and return to you." And Abraham took the wood of the burnt offering and laid it on Isaac his son, and he took in his hand the fire and the knife. So the two of them walked on together. And Isaac spoke to Abraham his father and said, "My father!" And he said, "Here I am,

1. This was a reasonable hope in Abraham's case, since God had promised to make a great nation from Isaac's line and Isaac had not yet produced any children.

2. The Hebrew verb stem used in the word *test* is used only here in all of Genesis. It's a stem that indicates the most intense meaning of the word. Although Abraham had faced many tests in his lifetime, this one was by far the most painful.

3. The Hebrew word for "burnt offering" is *ola.* It actually means "a whole burnt offering." The usual application was to an animal, and it meant for the animal to be burned completely, with nothing saved or held back.

> my son." And he said, "Behold, the fire and the wood, but where is the lamb for the burnt offering?" And Abraham said, "God will provide for Himself the lamb for the burnt offering, my son." So the two of them walked on together.
>
> Then they came to the place of which God had told him; and Abraham built the altar there, and arranged the wood, and bound his son Isaac, and laid him on the altar on top of the wood. And Abraham stretched out his hand, and took the knife to slay his son. (vv. 3–10)

Four things characterize Abraham's faith. First, *it was immediate.* Abraham didn't stew over his situation. He didn't postpone the inevitable by pacing the floor. He didn't worry and try to renegotiate with God. No excuses, no procrastination. His obedience rose bright and early in the morning.

Second, *it was characterized by confidence.* Did you catch that line in verse 5? "*We* will worship and return to you" (emphasis added). Now that's obstinate faith! He knew he was going up that mountain to kill his son, but he was just as sure he'd be bringing that son back alive. So confident was he that he viewed this expedition not as an act of teeth-gritting obedience, but as an opportunity for worship.

Third, *it was based on the character of God.* Could any question be more heart-wrenching than Isaac's in verse 7? "But Daddy, where's our animal?" This boy had offered up sacrifices with his father before. He knew the process; he knew something was missing. And his father gave the only possible reply. "God knows what we need. He'll give it to us at the right time."

What better response can we offer our own children in the face of need?

The fourth characteristic of Abraham's faith is that *it was thorough, not halfhearted.* Abraham didn't make any excuses, and he didn't leave himself an escape hatch. He didn't leave behind the materials for the altar; he didn't bring along a lamb just in case. He went as far as to bind his son and raise the knife. He planned to do it, and do it right.

But God came through.

> But the angel of the Lord called to him from heaven, and said, "Abraham, Abraham!" And he said, "Here I am." And he said, "Do not stretch out your hand against the lad, and do nothing to him; for now I know

> that you fear God, since you have not withheld your son, your only son, from Me." Then Abraham raised his eyes and looked, and behold, behind him a ram caught in the thicket by his horns; and Abraham went and took the ram, and offered him up for a burnt offering in the place of his son. (vv. 11–13)

"Now I know, and you know, Abraham. We know you fear Me more than you love him." The test was over, and Abraham had passed.

How was Abraham able to come through this difficult test with such flying colors? The answer is back in Hebrews 11:19.

> He *considered* that God is able to raise men even from the dead; from which he also received him back as a type.[4] (emphasis added)

The word *considered* means "to calculate, to reason, to take into account." And the idea is that, mentally, Abraham brought God into his reasoning. As he chose his response to this terrible test, he took into account all he knew about God.

An Example for Today

God hasn't asked us all for the kind of sacrifice He demanded from Abraham. But we each will face our own ultimate test, our own moment of truth regarding the condition of our hearts. And in that time, we will be glad we have remembered a few principles from Abraham's story.

God's Will Always Requires Obedience

It doesn't require understanding; it may not even make sense from a human standpoint. But it always requires obedience. Kick, scream, and fight all you want, but in the end, God will have His way.

God's Plan Is Never Fully Explained

We often forget this, but it's true. How often have you tried to second-guess God's intentions in the depths of your pain? How often have you cried an anguished *why* to a silent sky? Yet our heavenly Father doesn't explain the end at the beginning. He shows us only what He wants us to see.

4. The phrase "as a type" refers to Jesus Christ. This story is a perfect illustration of the Father offering up His Son, and then giving Him back for everyone to know of the peace and forgiveness and hope of God.

Our Response Invariably Reveals Our Theology

Whether you're a seminary graduate or you've never attended a Sunday school class, you have a personal *theology.* The word means "belief about God." When calamity strikes, when the bottom falls out, your theology will be the only thing left. And it will either be the life preserver that keeps you afloat or it will be the weights around your feet that pull you under.

A treadmill test can mean only a little perspiration on your forehead if you're in good shape. What kind of shape are your muscles of faith in? How steady is your pulse when a hurdle appears? Now's the time to build up your heart—before the speed on the treadmill is turned up and the test becomes strenuous.

Living Insights — STUDY ONE

For a parent, no story is more touching than the one about Abraham offering up Isaac. Truly, their experience was an ultimate test.

- Open your Bible to the story of Abraham and Isaac in Genesis 22:1–14. After you read through this passage, write it out in your own words. As you paraphrase, try to identify the emotions and feelings behind the words. Put yourself in Abraham's sandals . . . or Isaac's! Use this as a time to personalize the story.

Living Insights STUDY TWO

Tests are not partial—they eventually visit us all. Every Christian can give testimony of God's painful, yet purifying, hand in his or her life.

- What if Genesis 22 were blank in your Bible? Instead of the story of Abraham and Isaac, what if there were a space provided for *your* ultimate test? How would it read? Use this time today to write out your account of God's ultimate test in your life. Think of it as a journal entry, chronicling God's work in your life.

Chapter 5

FAITH SERVED FAMILY STYLE

Hebrews 11:20–23

Whatever else may be said about home, it is the bottom line of life, the anvil upon which attitudes and convictions are hammered out. It is the place where life's bills come due, the single most influential force in our earthly existence. No price tag can adequately reflect its value. No gauge can measure its ultimate influence . . . for good or ill. It is at home, among family members, that we come to terms with circumstances. It is here life makes up its mind."[1]

Although stripped of stained glass, soothing organ preludes, and the King's English, home is a sacred place. It's a place where milk is spilled, where toes are stubbed, and where people see you in your underwear.

It's real life . . . where real people rub up against real challenges. And how those people meet those challenges determines whether the faith of the family flourishes or flounders.

Faith for Family Living . . . and Dying

Faith is meant to be an everyday companion—not a weekend guest. In the curriculum of the Christian life, faith is a required course—not an elective. Our whole life should be lived on the basis of faith—not on the basis of just what we see. Because appearances are often deceiving, obscuring rather than clarifying things of eternal significance (2 Cor. 4:18). Faith gives us the clues to distinguish between the temporal and the eternal, between our earthly hut and our heavenly home (5:1–7).

Question: Where can we be most exposed to the contagious germs of faith?

Answer: The home. There is no place more riveted to reality.

With that in mind, let's peek through the keyholes of four homes to see faith being served up . . . family style.

1. Charles R. Swindoll, *Home: Where Life Makes Up Its Mind* (Portland, Oreg.: Multnomah Press, 1979), p. 5.

Faith in Four Homes

Hebrews 11:20–23 offers four glimpses into four different homes: Isaac's (v. 20), Jacob's (v. 21), Joseph's (v. 22), and Moses' (v. 23).

Isaac's Home

In verses 8–19, we saw Abraham and Sarah running with endurance the race of faith God had set before them. Now we see that baton of faith relayed to their son, who, in turn, passes it on to his sons.

> By faith Isaac blessed Jacob and Esau, even regarding things to come. (v. 20)

Isaac remembered the stories told him on his father's knee and his mother's lap. Stories of them leaving their homeland, "looking for the city which has foundations, whose architect and builder is God" (v. 10). Stories of living as aliens in a foreign land. Stories of his miraculous birth. Stories regarding things to come.

It was these latter stories that this aging patriarch strained to pass on to his boys, along with his blessing. The scene is preserved for us in Genesis 27–28. If we look beyond the deception and tragedy that color the scene, we find a tender moment of a father looking into the face of his son Jacob and blessing him. Even though his physical eyes were failing, Isaac's spiritual eyes could see the future with 20/20 vision. He saw a nation coming forth from Jacob's loins. A great nation. A respected nation. A nation chosen by God. All this Jacob learned from his father, who, in turn, had learned it from his.

Do you have a godly father or mother? If so, it's a rich heritage you should treasure. Take a minute to reflect on your memories of your parents. These memories may not all be picture perfect—neither was the scrapbook of Abraham and Sarah, by the way—but if they passed on to you any measure of faith, that's a lot to be thankful for. Why not pause here to reflect on specific moments with your parents and thank God for the heritage He blessed you with.

Jacob's Home

Let's skip over several decades and take a peek through the keyhole of Jacob's front door.

> By faith Jacob, as he was dying, blessed each of the sons of Joseph, and worshiped, leaning on the top of his staff. (Heb. 11:21)

The summary in Hebrews 11 is taken from the incident found in Genesis 48, where Jacob pronounced a benediction over Ephraim and Manasseh.

"The angel who has redeemed me from all evil,
Bless the lads;
And may my name live on in them,
And the names of my fathers Abraham and Isaac;
And may they grow into a multitude in the midst of
the earth." (v. 16)

Here we have the example of a grandfather passing on a blessing to his grandsons. Did you have a godly grandparent? Someone who told you Bible stories and recollections of how God had worked in his or her life? Someone who prayed with you . . . and for you? Someone who was a blessing to you? If so, you have a great heritage and much to be thankful for.

Look through the eyes of this third grader who wrote "What's A Grandmother?" and see if it doesn't bring thanks to your lips—and maybe even a tear to your eye.

> A grandmother is a lady who has no children of her own. She likes other people's little girls and boys. A grandfather is a man grandmother. He goes for walks with the boys, and they talk about fishing and stuff like that.
>
> Grandmothers don't have to do anything except to be there. They're old so they shouldn't play hard or run. It is enough if they drive us to the market where the pretend horse is, and have a lot of dimes ready. Or if they take us for walks, they should slow down past things like pretty leaves and caterpillars. They should never say "hurry-up."
>
> Usually grandmothers are fat, but not too fat to tie your shoes. They wear glasses and funny underwear. They can take their teeth and gums off.
>
> Grandmothers don't have to be smart, only answer questions like, "Why isn't God married?" and "How come dogs chase cats!"
>
> Grandmothers don't talk baby talk like visitors do, because it is hard to understand. When they read to us they don't skip or mind if it is the same story over again.
>
> Everybody should try to have a grandmother, especially if you don't have television, because they are the only grown-ups who have time.[2]

2. As quoted by James Dobson in *What Wives Wish Their Husbands Knew about Women* (Wheaton, Ill.: Tyndale House Publishers, Living Books, 1975), p. 48.

Joseph's Home

The next keyhole we'll look through lets us catch a conversation not from father to son or grandfather to grandson but from brother to brother.

> By faith Joseph, when he was dying, made mention of the exodus of the sons of Israel, and gave orders concerning his bones. (Heb. 11:22)

The original scene is preserved for us in Genesis 50:24–25.

> And Joseph said to his brothers, "I am about to die, but God will surely take care of you, and bring you up from this land to the land which He promised on oath to Abraham, to Isaac and to Jacob." Then Joseph made the sons of Israel swear, saying, "God will surely take care of you, and you shall carry my bones up from here."

Joseph was an Egyptian by geography and by virtue of his occupation, but he was an Israelite by heritage and by the dictates of his heart. And when he died, he didn't want to end up in some pagan pyramid; he wanted his bones buried with the people of promise.[3]

How did Joseph know of God's promise to the nation of Israel? He had been told about it by Jacob, who had been told by Isaac, who had been told by Abraham. What is a family? "It is a perpetual relay of truth,"[4] says Edith Schaeffer. Whatever your past heritage, savor the encouraging words she has to say about the importance of your link to future generations.

> One person in one family in one village in one county in one nation can, even *alone*, be the one to start the beginning of a new line of believers, as that one begins to really pray for specific individuals, to talk when the moment opens up, and to lead a few others one by one to know true truth. . . .
>
> Can't you imagine them now? Throughout all centuries, all geographic locations—some from every tribe and nation and kindred and tongue and people—being faithful, handing the flag of true truth, not dropping out, starting new family lines—right up to the moment when Jesus comes back again![5]

3. The fulfillment of Joseph's request is recorded in Exodus 13:19.

4. Edith Schaeffer, *What Is a Family?* (Old Tappan, N.J.: Fleming H. Revell Co., Power Books, 1975), p. 119.

5. Schaeffer, *What Is a Family?*, p. 147.

Moses' Home

Our final stop is at the door of Moses.

> By faith Moses, when he was born, was hidden for three months by his parents, because they saw he was a beautiful child; and they were not afraid of the king's edict. (Heb. 11:23)

It was the paranoia of Pharaoh that prompted the slaughter of Hebrew infants, whom he feared would strengthen the nation that one day might rise up against him. Exodus 1 records the program of persecution and the heroism of the Hebrew midwives in defying the king's edict. Exodus 2 focuses on one particular child—Moses—who was saved from the slaughter.

By faith, a husband and a wife conspired together against the oppressive fist of Pharaoh to save their son from death—and save him for a glorious future as deliverer of the enslaved nation.

How about Your Home?

Let's leave the ancient homes of these people who lived by faith and head toward your neighborhood. Let's stop at *your* house . . . take a peek through the keyhole of *your* front door. What will we see?

For faith to be served up family style, nourishing generations to come, two things need to happen. First, we must think of our homes as training bases—not holding pens; the home should be a launching pad for sending children into the world—not a storage facility for isolating them from it. Second, we must develop in our homes a contagious confidence in God—not a demoralizing determination to endure; the home should be the anvil upon which our faith is forged—not a vat of cold water where it is quenched.

Truly, home is the place where life makes up its mind. But what it makes up its mind about is entirely up to you. And that's a pretty sobering responsibility.

Living Insights STUDY ONE

Faith was never meant to remain theoretical. It was intended to be translated into reality.

- With the assistance of a Bible concordance, conduct a Scripture search on the word *faith* in the New Testament. Copy down any insightful references and personalize them in an applicational summary.

Faith	
Verse	Applicational Summary

Living Insights

STUDY TWO

How's the faith where you live? Is it healthy and vibrant, or a bit sickly and weak? Take this time to do some personal evaluation.

- We learned that we should think of our homes as training bases, not holding pens.

  In what ways is your home like a training base?

  ____

  ____

  ____

In what ways is your home like a holding pen?

____

____

____

- We also learned that our homes should be characterized by contagious confidence in God, not a demoralizing determination to endure.

  Confidence in God is caught by repeated exposure rather than taught by repeated exposition. How do you demonstrate contagious confidence in God?

  ____

  ____

  ____

  Many people coming out of Christian homes seem defeated before they've even been sent out to battle. Whether by precept or by example, they've been taught that the Christian life is not something you enjoy but something you endure. Is there a demoralizing determination to endure in your home? In what areas does it appear?

  ____

  ____

  ____

Chapter 6

Moses' Faith, Moses' Choices . . . and Me

Hebrews 11:24–28

In his excellent biography of Moses, F. B. Meyer describes the life and times of this illustrious leader who grew up in the cushioned lap of Egyptian royalty.

> What a magnificent land must Egypt have been in those days of which Herodotus and the hieroglyphic records speak! The atmosphere was rainless; the Nile brought from afar the rich alluvial soil, that bore corn enough to feed the world; the banks of the river were covered with cities, villages, stately temples, and all the evidences of an advanced civilization; whilst mighty pyramids and colossal figures towered to a hundred feet in height. . . .
>
> *The cream of all this was poured into the cup of* Moses. He was brought up in the palace, and treated as the grandson of Pharaoh. If he rode forth into the streets, it would be in a princely equipage, amid the cries of "Bow the knee." If he floated on the Nile, it would be in a golden barge, amid the strains of voluptuous music. If he wished for aught, the almost illimitable wealth of the treasures of Egypt was within his reach.
>
> When old enough he was probably sent to be *educated in the college,* which had grown up around the Temple of the Sun, and has been called "the Oxford of Ancient Egypt." There he would learn to read and write the mysterious heiroglyph; there, too, he would be instructed in mathematics, astronomy, and chemistry, in all of which the Egyptians were adepts. . . .
>
> But Moses was something more than a royal student, spending his years in cultured refinement and lettered ease. *He was a statesman and a soldier.* . . . Josephus says that whilst he was still in his early manhood the Ethiopians invaded Egypt, routed the army sent against them, and threatened Memphis [the capital]. In the panic the oracles were consulted; and on their recommendation Moses was entrusted with the

> command of the royal troops. He immediately took the field, surprised and defeated the enemy, captured their principal city, "the swamp-engirdled city of Meroë," and returned to Egypt laden with the spoils of victory.[1]

Today we want to take a look at this man Moses—at his faith, his decisions, and how they relate to you and me several millennia later.

Three Risky Decisions: Moses' Faith in Operation

The monument to Moses erected in Hebrews 11 is the only one you'll find. No hieroglyphed tomb records his deeds. No quarried pyramid remembers his death. Why? Because of three risky decisions that showed his faith but alienated him from his peers.

Refusal to Sustain the Sinful

Although Moses' home was in the palace, his heart was with the people of God. And as he grew older, the dictates of his heart determined his destiny.

> By faith Moses, when he had grown up, refused to be called the son of Pharaoh's daughter; choosing rather to endure ill-treatment with the people of God, than to enjoy the passing pleasures of sin; considering the reproach of Christ greater riches than the treasures of Egypt; for he was looking to the reward. (vv. 24–26)

Picture the tormented Moses—Hebrew within, Egyptian without—wrestling with the tension of embracing the material at the expense of the spiritual. His decision was not made in the haste of one trying to write himself into the history books. He already had greatness and respect and notoriety. Nor was the decision made in some adolescent crest of emotion that broke over him and swept him away. It was the measured and mature decision of an adult—something he *chose* (v. 25) and *considered* (v. 26).

The mental picture in verse 25 is of a fork in the road that placed him on the tines of a difficult decision. The road that veered left was paved with golden opportunities "to enjoy the passing pleasures of sin." The road that went off to the right was potholed with uncertain footing, which would lead him "to endure ill-treatment with the people of God."

1. F. B. Meyer, *Moses: The Servant of God* (New York, N.Y.: Fleming H. Revell Co., n.d.), pp. 18–19.

His choice of roads was determined by what he considered. The Greek word for *considering* in verse 26 means "to lead, to go before, to think." Moses thought ahead. He looked down the road to where his decision would take him. And what did he discover? That in eternity's balance, the reward for enduring the reproach of Christ outweighed the experience of enjoying anything Egypt had to offer.

Moses was looking past the fence line that bounded earth's limits to heaven's greener pastures. He had his eyes fixed on the reward. And so what he gave up became blurred in the periphery, and what he would ultimately gain came into clear focus.

Anyone who refuses to sustain the sinful must go through a similar process. That can't be done with a fixation on ephemeral pleasures, regardless of how iridescent or irresistible. Every day we are faced with a fork in the road—one way to Egypt . . . the other to Christ. The decisions we make at those crossroads will determine whether we end up entombed in some pyramid or elevated to faith's hall of fame.

Determination to Leave the Familiar

Underlying the economy of words in verse 27 is a wealth of emotion.

> By faith he left Egypt, not fearing the wrath of the king; for he endured, as seeing Him who is unseen.

Moses knew Egypt better than any place on earth. His name was a household word at the dinner tables of the populace. He knew the streets and the buildings and the monuments. He was familiar with the sights and sounds and smells. Such security. Such comfortable, predictable familiarity. Yet, by faith, he determined to leave all that behind.

That decision took backbone—"not fearing the wrath of the king." And it took vision—"seeing Him who is unseen."

The life of faith is a pilgrimage, not a pasture. Either we venture or we vegetate. Either we risk or we rust.

Willingness to Do the Unusual

The third decision noted in Hebrews 11 marks Moses as a pioneer willing to venture into uncharted territory.

> By faith he kept the Passover and the sprinkling of the blood, so that he who destroyed the first-born might not touch them. (v. 28)

Nothing else in Israel's worship was quite as unusual as this ritual. Paint the Passover scene in your mind with the bold colors from Exodus 12:5–13.

> "'Your lamb shall be an unblemished male a year old; you may take it from the sheep or from the goats. And you shall keep it until the fourteenth day of the same month, then the whole assembly of the congregation of Israel is to kill it at twilight. Moreover, they shall take some of the blood and put it on the two doorposts and on the lintel of the houses in which they eat it. And they shall eat the flesh that same night, roasted with fire, and they shall eat it with unleavened bread and bitter herbs. Do not eat any of it raw or boiled at all with water, but rather roasted with fire, both its head and its legs along with its entrails. And you shall not leave any of it over until morning, but whatever is left of it until morning, you shall burn with fire. Now you shall eat it in this manner: with your loins girded, your sandals on your feet, and your staff in your hand; and you shall eat it in haste—it is the Lord's Passover. For I will go through the land of Egypt on that night, and will strike down all the first-born in the land of Egypt, both man and beast; and against all the gods of Egypt I will execute judgments—I am the Lord. And the blood shall be a sign for you on the houses where you live; and when I see the blood I will pass over you, and no plague will befall you to destroy you when I strike the land of Egypt.'"

Do you see what's so unusual? Here's Moses, a brilliant man, well educated, and he's in front of his dwelling, smearing blood on the doorposts. How incongruous to his upbringing. How unusual.

Yet *unusual* is the company faith seems to prefer. Moses' actions were about as unusual as Noah building an ark without a cloud in the sky . . . as unusual as Abraham and Sarah taking childbirth classes when they were pushing the century mark—as unusual as Isaac lying on the altar with the blade in his father's hand, glinting in the sun.

Is God asking you to go down an unusual road too? A road that's uncertain, even precarious? If so, you have to decide: Do I want a monument in Egypt—or a reward in heaven?

That decision will determine your destiny.

How about You and Me Today?

Life can seem like a forest of confusion, woven with winding rabbit trails. But when you really think about it, there are always only two roads that stretch before us: the heavily trafficked highway to Egypt and the less-traveled road to heaven.

To travel the road of faith means making some pretty risky decisions. Here are some road signs to point you in the right direction and to keep you on the right path.

- To have the discernment it takes to refuse the sinful,
  faith must overshadow my feelings.
- To have the determination it takes to leave the familiar,
  faith must be my security.
- To have the discipline it takes to do the unusual,
  faith must silence my critics.

Moses made three decisions. He refused the sinful (Heb. 11:24–26). He left the familiar (v. 27). He did the unusual (v. 28). And those three decisions made all the difference, determining not only the course his life would take, but whether he would rot in Egypt or be rewarded in heaven.

Which road will you choose?

Living Insights STUDY ONE

In the world's eyes, Moses could have had it all. But he chose "ill-treatment . . . considering the reproach of Christ greater riches." He presents us with an approach to faith worth emulating.

- We are all tempted to enjoy sin's passing pleasures. Perhaps having a passage like this in the back of our minds would help us fight the flesh. So let's memorize Hebrews 11:24–26. These three verses flow together into one challenging thought. Begin your memorization by reading the verses aloud several times. After a dozen readings, you'll begin to feel the passage etching itself into your mind.

Living Insights STUDY TWO

This study taught us that faith involves refusing the sinful, leaving the familiar, and doing the unusual. Where are you in all of this?

- Discernment, determination, and discipline are practical outgrowths of faith. Are these three elements evident in your faith? Let's use today's Living Insights for prayer. Talk to your Father about your faith. Speak about your strengths and weaknesses, and ask Him for help in improving areas of need.

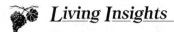

Chapter 7

By Faith, Miracles!

Hebrews 11:29–31

Intimidation. That is what made the Israelite spies cower like grasshoppers before the giants in Canaan (Num. 13:32–33). That is what made their palms sweat, their knees knock, and their feet want to turn back.

We may have those same feelings as we come to Hebrews 11, where portraits of storied giants of faith hang in massive, ornate frames, gilded with the accumulated admiration of the centuries. Walking through that marbled Hall of Fame, we can hear the hollow echo of our own footsteps . . . and we have a naked awareness that we, too, are merely grasshoppers by comparison.

Intimidation will do a number on us if we let it. But today's lesson will keep that from happening, helping us walk down that hall and letting those portraits inspire us—not intimidate us.

Some Essential and Encouraging Reminders

It's hard to identify with a man who spends a hundred years building a barge, a woman who conceives at age ninety, a man whose outstretched hand is poised to sacrifice his only son, or an eighty-year-old man who pioneers an exodus and pastors a congregation of two million nomads. It seems that you'd need a pretty potent pedigree to breed that kind of faith. Yet here you are feeling like a mutt, whimpering and scratching on heaven's door for a scrap of faith just to get you through the day.

If that's how you feel when you rub shoulders with the Hebrews 11 crowd, we have three essential reminders to encourage you.

First: *People are people—nothing more.* The world isn't divided into supersaints and Clark Kent Christians, those who can leap tall buildings in a single bound of faith and those who can't jump to a conclusion without tripping over a minor premise. Every person in the family of God is just P.O.H.—Plain Old Humanity. Each of us is poured from the same bottle of plain vanilla extract, nothing exquisite or extravagant. We're all just people in plain paper wrapping.

Second: *God is God—nothing less.* He's the same yesterday, today, and forever (Heb. 13:8). He hasn't changed since the time of Noah or Abraham or Moses, and He's no less involved with our lives than He was with theirs. David speaks of this involvement in his prayer in Psalm 139.

> O Lord, Thou hast searched me and known me.
> Thou dost know when I sit down and when I rise up;
> Thou dost understand my thought from afar.
> Thou dost scrutinize my path and my lying down,
> And art intimately acquainted with all my ways.
> (vv. 1–3)

More than three thousand years later, an echo of God's intimate involvement can be heard in John Baillie's prayer: "O God of mercy, who so carest for me as if Thou hadst none else to care for, yet carest for all even as Thou carest for me . . ."[1]

Once you come to grips with the truths of these prayers, intimidation will flee from your life like a shadow before the noonday sun.

Third: *Miracles are miracles—nothing else.* C. S. Lewis defines *miracle* as "an interference with Nature by supernatural power."[2] It is a humanly impossible event that occurs in the natural realm, apart from natural causes, for the purpose of glorifying God. If a miracle is authentic, it defies human explanation or duplication.[3]

A miracle can occur anyplace, anytime, and to anyone. Miracles of the Bible were performed in Egypt, in the wilderness, and in the Promised Land. They were experienced in the time of the Old Covenant as well as in the time of the New. They happened to widows (1 Kings 17) as well as to wise men (Matt. 2:1–12). Miracles can be as public as the parting of the Red Sea or as private as the divine conception within Mary's womb.

They are, however, the exception rather than the rule—a foretaste of the kingdom rather than the feast itself.

Three True and Miraculous Accounts

Turning our attention to Hebrews 11:29–31, we encounter three miracles of incredible magnitude involving the waters of a sea, the walls of a city, and the welcome of a harlot.

1. John Baillie, *A Diary of Private Prayer* (New York, N.Y.: Charles Scribner's Sons, 1977), p. 67.

2. C. S. Lewis, *Miracles* (New York, N.Y.: Macmillan Co., 1947), p. 10.

3. The healing of the man born blind in John 9 is a perfect example. That miracle glorified God (vv. 3, 38) and defied human explanation and duplication (vv. 19, 26, 32).

The Waters of a Sea

Thousands of years after the fact, Hebrews 11:29 records the seismic aftershocks of an event that shook the world.

> By faith [the Israelites] passed through the Red Sea as though they were passing through dry land; and the Egyptians, when they attempted it, were drowned.

The original record of the episode is found in Exodus 14. Let's look at a few verses from this account, noting particularly the nature of the people, the nature of God, and the nature of the miracle.

> And as Pharaoh drew near, the sons of Israel looked, and behold, the Egyptians were marching after them, and they became very frightened; so the sons of Israel cried out to the Lord. Then they said to Moses, "Is it because there were no graves in Egypt that you have taken us away to die in the wilderness? Why have you dealt with us in this way, bringing us out of Egypt? Is this not the word that we spoke to you in Egypt, saying, 'Leave us alone that we may serve the Egyptians'? For it would have been better for us to serve the Egyptians than to die in the wilderness." . . .
>
> Then the Lord said to Moses, "Why are you crying out to Me? Tell the sons of Israel to go forward. And as for you, lift up your staff and stretch out your hand over the sea and divide it, and the sons of Israel shall go through the midst of the sea on dry land. And as for Me, behold, I will harden the hearts of the Egyptians so that they will go in after them; and I will be honored through Pharaoh and all his army, through his chariots and his horsemen." (vv. 10–12, 15–17)

If you were picking members for your team to demonstrate faith, it's doubtful that these Israelites would be anywhere in the ballpark, let alone be your first-round draft picks. They complained, panicked, doubted, were fearful, blamed their leader, and wanted to retreat (vv. 10–14). Hardly Hall of Fame material. And hardly anyone for us to be intimidated by.

But how about the Lord? Was He distant, like some deist conception of God? Not on your life. He was aware. He was involved (vv. 15–20). And He intervened with a miracle (vv. 21–22).

The Walls of a City

Hebrews 11:30 capsulizes the second miracle for us.

> By faith the walls of Jericho fell down, after they had been encircled for seven days.

Forty years after the crossing of the Red Sea, the Israelites crossed the Jordan into the Promised Land. By that time, disobedience had disqualified Moses to lead the people over, and he had chosen as his successor a stalwart leader named Joshua. With the divine mandate to take the land, Joshua rallied his troops under the unfurling flag of faith before their first military target—the bastion of Jericho, a small but heavily fortified, high-walled city.

Talk about intimidation. Here we have a ragged fray of foot soldiers who are grossly outnumbered and scratching their heads about the strategy given them to conquer that Canaanite citadel.

Joshua 6 records in detail the battle plan God handed them.

> Now Jericho was tightly shut because of the sons of Israel; no one went out and no one came in. And the Lord said to Joshua, "See, I have given Jericho into your hand, with its king and the valiant warriors. And you shall march around the city, all the men of war circling the city once. You shall do so for six days. Also seven priests shall carry seven trumpets of rams' horns before the ark; then on the seventh day you shall march around the city seven times, and the priests shall blow the trumpets. And it shall be that when they make a long blast with the ram's horn, and when you hear the sound of the trumpet, all the people shall shout with a great shout; and the wall of the city will fall down flat, and the people will go up every man straight ahead." (vv. 1–5)

March around the wall seven times . . . blow a long time on the horns . . . and after that, everybody scream their lungs out. "Yeah, right, Lord," you can almost hear the troops mumble under their breath. It was hardly the strategy you'd find in a West Point textbook. But it was God's strategy . . . and God is God. And the plan unfolded the way He said it would (vv. 12–16, 20–21).

Those outnumbered Israelites, weary from years of wandering in the wilderness, pulled off a major military upset. How? Simply by believing that God could do the miraculous.

The Welcome of a Harlot

Amidst the rubble of Jericho's tumbled walls, it's easy to overlook the less spectacular miracle found in Hebrews 11:31.

> By faith Rahab the harlot did not perish along with those who were disobedient, after she had welcomed the spies in peace.

The Hall of Famer in this case is not a Sarah, the mother of the Jewish people, or a Mary, the mother of Christ . . . but a prostitute. We should certainly experience no intimidation here.

Rahab was a resident of Jericho who aided and abetted the Hebrew spies before the city was destroyed (Josh. 2). From her testimony to the spies it is clear she had faith in God.

> "I know perfectly well that your God is going to give my country to you," she told them. "We are all afraid of you; everyone is terrified if the word *Israel* is even mentioned. For we have heard how the Lord made a path through the Red Sea for you when you left Egypt! . . . Your God is the supreme God of heaven, not just an ordinary god. Now I beg for this one thing: Swear to me by the sacred name of your God that when Jericho is conquered you will let me live, along with my father and mother, my brothers and sisters, and all their families. This is only fair after the way I have helped you." (vv. 9–10a, 11b–13)[4]

The miracle was that when the walls of the city collapsed, Rahab's home, which sat atop the wall, remained intact (compare Josh. 2:15 with 6:20, 22).

Her untouched home, arising out of the debris of Jericho's razed walls, stood like a monument to her faith. In response to that faith God rewarded her not only by granting deliverance from the destruction (6:22–25) but by grafting her into the family tree of the eagerly awaited Messiah (Matt. 1:5).

Present-Day Miracles of Faith

Don't think that these miraculous events are porcelain pieces in museum settings to be oohed and aahed at from a safe, cordoned-off distance.

People are still people. God is still God. And miracles are still miracles.

Are you needing a miracle? Is your back against some Red Sea? Do you hear the angry hoofbeats of some approaching army? *Count*

4. The Living Bible (Wheaton, Ill.: Tyndale House Publishers, 1971).

on Him to get you through and make a way of escape. He specializes in parting seas—no matter how deep, how wide, how turbulent.

Are you facing some intimidating wall that is looming before you? Maybe it's a wall of resistance at work or the stony silence of an offended friend. *Wait on Him to penetrate the walls of defense.* He specializes in tearing down walls—even through the most unconventional of strategies.

Are you plagued with a checkered past? None was more checkered than Rahab's. Yet God delivered her, not only from destruction but from her past. *Trust in Him to restore your worth in the eyes of others.* He specializes in helping harlots and rebuilding the walls of ruined reputations.

Living Insights

STUDY ONE

We have here three more champions of faith: Moses, Joshua, and Rahab. These are very diverse folks, yet all are characterized by one essential ingredient—faith. Let's get to know them better.

- Take a few minutes to examine each character in the particular settings we studied in our lesson. As you read their stories, create a character sketch of each one. Granted, the sketches will be brief, but try to pack them full!

Moses: Exodus 14

Joshua: Joshua 6

Rahab: Joshua 2, 6:22–25

Living Insights STUDY TWO

In the lives of these three characters, do you see resemblances to your own life? Are there lessons you can learn from the stories of these faithful people?

- Which of these three words best describes how you felt in a recent difficult situation?

  Pressured   Defensive   Worthless

- In view of your first answer, which character can you best relate to?

  Moses   Joshua   Rahab

- Jot down three or four lessons you can learn from the life of this biblical character—so that he or she can help you with your struggles.

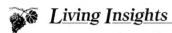

Chapter 8

TRIUMPHS AND TRAGEDIES OF THE FAITHFUL

Hebrews 11:32–40

There's a story told of a Quaker who owned an ornery milk cow. Every time he milked the cow, he was faced with the problem of its disposition. Bright and early one morning things came to a head. While the Quaker was milking, the cow reached over and bumped the bucket. Out poured the milk all over the Quaker's shoes and the bottom of his overalls. This otherwise passive Quaker set the bucket upright rather firmly and began to milk again. Didn't say anything. A few moments later the cow reached back and stepped right on the man's foot, grinding her hoof down into his toe. The Quaker looked at the cow and frowned but said nothing. He merely bit his lip and kept on milking. Then the cow reared back and kicked this fellow about fifteen feet. That did it. He walked over, stood in front of the cow, and said, "Thou knowest that I am a Quaker. And thou knowest that I cannot strike thee back—but I can sell thee to a Presbyterian!"

Funny story, but it illustrates an important point.

There *are* times when we must turn the other cheek, but there are also times when we must stand up to wrong, fight back, or—in the case of the Quaker—sell.

Erroneous Ideas about the Christian Life

Many people are plagued with misconceptions about how Christians should act and feel and be. These misconceptions fall into four different categories and are voiced by Christians and non-Christians alike.

- *Regarding passivity:* Christians are followers of Jesus; therefore, they should be meek, mild, and passive.
- *Regarding persistence:* Christians are people of faith; therefore, they should never doubt or become discouraged.
- *Regarding perfection:* Christians are totally forgiven and are new creatures in Christ (2 Cor. 5:17); therefore, they are free from their humanity and the marks of imperfection.

- *Regarding protection:* Christians know God; therefore, they are shielded from hardship, calamity, and tragedy.

Strip away the veneer of these smooth-sounding ideas about the Christian life, however, and you can see how flimsy the particleboard reasoning really is.

Let's look at them one by one. First, Jesus stood firm against His critics; He wasn't passive and He didn't allow people to walk all over Him (see Matt. 23). Second, Christians are human and, like anyone else, teeter from time to time on the brink of uncertainty; some even fall headlong into the deepest and darkest of depressions (see Ps. 31:9–13). Third, Christians still have a sin nature after they've been born again, so they still struggle with sin (see Rom. 7:7–25). Fourth, Christians can and do experience calamities of every kind. Bad things *do* happen to forgiven people, a fact we are reminded of in the last nine verses of Hebrews 11.

Actual Examples of Endurance

The theme of Hebrews 11 is *endurance.* In this chapter we see paraded before us the persevering faith of generations who trusted God against all laws of logic, against all odds, and against prevailing public opinion.

As we've already seen in our first lesson, Hebrews 10:32–39 underscores the need for endurance.

> But remember the former days, when, after being enlightened, you endured a great conflict of sufferings, partly, by being made a public spectacle through reproaches and tribulations, and partly by becoming sharers with those who were so treated. For you showed sympathy to the prisoners, and accepted joyfully the seizure of your property, knowing that you have for yourselves a better possession and an abiding one. Therefore, do not throw away your confidence, which has a great reward. For you have need of endurance, so that when you have done the will of God, you may receive what was promised.
>
> For yet in a very little while,
> He who is coming will come, and will
> not delay.
> But My righteous one shall live by faith;
> And if he shrinks back, My soul has no
> pleasure in him.

> But we are not of those who shrink back to destruction,
> but of those who have faith to the preserving of the soul.

In chapter 11, the writer puts flesh and blood on the skeleton of his exhortation to endure.

Historic Names and Roles

A visit to the Viet Nam Memorial in Washington, D.C., is an emotional one. This horizontal monolith stretches across a park, its polished darkness bearing the names of nearly fifty-eight thousand Americans who lost their lives in the war. Its impact lies in its simplicity. There is no monumental sculpture, no eulogy of stirring words chiseled into stone. Simply row after row of the names of those who died.

Hebrews 11:32–40 stretches before us in similar truncated eloquence.

> And what more shall I say? For time will fail me if I tell of Gideon, Barak, Samson, Jephthah, of David and Samuel and the prophets. (v. 32)

If the list continued today, it would include the Corrie ten Booms, the Jim Elliots, the Hudson Taylors, the homemakers and the professionals, the teenagers and the senior citizens. Not one of them perfect . . . or passive . . . or totally persistent . . . or protected from the sharp corners of life.

Illustrations of Two Extremes

The peaks and valleys of Christian experience are landscaped for us in verses 33–38. As we stroll through these verses, we must do so with the reverence of one walking through Arlington National Cemetery or standing before the Viet Nam Memorial. For it is sacred ground where the faithful are eulogized—not just a doctrinal treatise.

Triumphs of the faithful. Verses 33–35a stand in the text as an awe-inspiring mountain range jutting triumphantly skyward.

> Who by faith conquered kingdoms, performed acts of righteousness, obtained promises, shut the mouths of lions, quenched the power of fire, escaped the edge of the sword, from weakness were made strong, became mighty in war, put foreign armies to flight. Women received back their dead by resurrection.

Tragedies of the faithful. Juxtaposed to the peaks in those verses is a precipitous slide into dark valleys of tragedy in verses 35b–38.

> And others were tortured, not accepting their release, in order that they might obtain a better resurrection;[1] and others experienced mockings and scourgings, yes, also chains and imprisonment. They were stoned, they were sawn in two, they were tempted, they were put to death with the sword; they went about in sheepskins, in goatskins, being destitute, afflicted, ill-treated (men of whom the world was not worthy), wandering in deserts and mountains and caves and holes in the ground.

Just as life-giving rain falls on the just and the unjust, so life-threatening storms sweep over the righteous as well as the wicked. Bad things do happen to good people, a truth to which *Fox's Book of Martyrs* bears testimony.

> It has been said that the lives of the early Christians consisted of "persecution above ground and prayer below ground." Their lives are expressed by the Coliseum and the catacombs. Beneath Rome are the excavations which we call the catacombs, which were at once temples and tombs. The early Church of Rome might well be called the Church of the Catacombs. There are some sixty catacombs near Rome, in which some six hundred miles of galleries have been traced, and these are not all. These galleries are about eight feet high and from three to five feet wide, containing on either side several rows of long, low, horizontal recesses, one above another like berths in a ship. In these the dead bodies were placed and the front closed, either by a single marble slab or several great tiles laid in mortar. On these slabs or tiles, epitaphs or symbols are graved or painted. Both pagans and Christians buried their dead in these catacombs. When the Christian graves have been opened, the skeletons tell their own terrible tale. Heads are found severed from the body, ribs and shoulder blades are broken, bones are often calcined from fire.[2]

1. One commentator explains this phrase this way: "Mention is now made of *some* who *were tortured, refusing to accept release, that they might rise again to a better life,* that is to say, that they might experience a resurrection better than a reprieve from death at the hand of their tormentors and in this sense the restoration to life which was offered them if they would deny their faith in God." Philip Edgcumbe Hughes, *A Commentary on the Epistle to the Hebrews* (Grand Rapids, Mich.: William B. Eerdmans Publishing Co., 1977), p. 512.

2. William Byron Forbush, ed., *Fox's Book of Martyrs* (Grand Rapids, Mich.: Zondervan Publishing House, 1967), p. 11.

Effects Then and Now

Verses 39–40 summarize the experiences of the triumphant and the tragic.

> And all these, having gained approval through their faith, did not receive what was promised, because God had provided something better for us, so that apart from us they should not be made perfect.

God didn't grade these believers on the basis of how successful their lives were but how faithful. They "gained approval through their faith." And the promise they longed to see, we have seen and heard and touched in the Lord Jesus Christ. They lived by a faith that looked into the dim, distant future, while we live by a faith that looks back two thousand years with crystal clarity.

Those ancient saints form our spiritual family tree. Without them, we have no roots. Without us, they have no branches. They are "made perfect," or *completed,* as the life-giving sap of their lives flows through our spiritual leaves and flowers to fill the earth with the fragrance of faith.

Practical Impact Today

In the drama of redemption, God has included triumph as well as tragedy. There are those who stand center stage, bathed in the limelight, who thrill us with their heroic deeds and satisfy us with their lives lived happily ever after. Then there are those whose lives are plotted with pain on a downwardly sloped story line to tragedy.

It's important to note that undeserving and sinful Christians often experience unexpected triumphs. It's also important to note that godly and deserving Christians often must endure the plot twists of unexplained tragedies. Both extremes link us with the uninterrupted historical drama we call "God's Plan." God is the playwright. We are the actors on stage.

So whatever role you have been scripted to play, play it well, play it with all your heart . . . because you only have a brief moment on that stage.

Living Insights STUDY ONE

One of the finest privileges enjoyed by a Christian is the opportunity to personally study the Word of God. Let's dig deeper into the richness of the eleventh chapter of Hebrews.

- Write down the cross references in the margin of your Bible that relate to the people and incidents mentioned in verses 32–40. As you enter them in the following chart, take some time to read through those references and see in detail how God uses triumphs and tragedies in the unfolding drama of the lives of those He loves.

People and Incidents	Cross References
Gideon	Judges 6–8
Barak	
Samson	
Jephthah	
David	
Samuel	
"Conquered kingdoms"	
"Performed acts of righteousness"	
"Obtained promises"	
"Shut the mouths of lions"	
"Quenched the power of fire"	
"Escaped the edge of the sword"	
"Became mighty in war"	
"Put foreign armies to flight"	
"Women received back their dead by resurrection"	
"Chains and imprisonment"	
"Stoned"	
"Sawn in two"	
"Put to death with the sword"	
"Went about in sheepskins, in goatskins, being destitute, afflicted"	
"Ill-treated"	
"Wandering in deserts and mountains and caves and holes in the ground"	

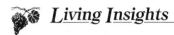

Living Insights STUDY TWO

How are you at handling the ironies of life? Today's study dealt with two paradoxes. Why not bring together your family or a group of close friends and discuss the following questions.

- How do you respond when you see sinful Christians experiencing triumphs?
- What type of response does the Scripture teach us? Support your answer with specific verses.
- How do you respond when godly Christians suffer tragedy?
- What type of response does the Bible teach us? Again, support your answer with specific references.
- Have you personally experienced either of these conditions? Can you describe the feelings you had while it was going on?

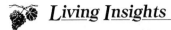

Chapter 9

ARENA LIFESTYLE

Hebrews 12:1–3

The New Testament often describes the Christian life as a race to be run or a fight to be fought. These metaphors stem from the literal reality of the athletic events that were conducted in ancient arenas.

> Physical training was an important part of Greek education and centered in the gymnasium. . . . Foot races were held in the stadium (Gk. *stadion*, a distance of about two hundred yards). Several of these stadia still survive with their starting and finish lines (cf. the mark or goal in Phil. 3:14). The Greek stadia accommodated spectators on the grassy slopes on each side of the flat running surfaces.
>
> The major sports were running, boxing, the *pankration* (an all-out combination of boxing, wrestling, and kicking in which no holds were barred except for biting and gouging), and the pentathlon (which included running, long-jumping, throwing the discus, throwing the javelin, and wrestling).[1]

Becoming a Christian means we enter an arena where there is pain, heartache, sickness, sorrow, pressure, hardship, and even death. It is there we run against formidable competition. It is there that our mettle is tested.

If we are to be victorious in the arena of real life, we need endurance and encouragement. That is why we have the roster of Hebrews 11, listing those who ran the race with endurance and cleared the high hurdles placed in their paths.

Audience Surrounding the Arena

As we come to chapter 12, we see these same spiritual athletes ushered off the track and into the grandstands, figuratively cheering us on with their encouraging testimonies, as we carry on the Olympic tradition of enduring faith.

1. Everett Ferguson, *Backgrounds of Early Christianity* (Grand Rapids, Mich.: William B. Eerdmans Publishing Co., 1987), p. 76.

> Therefore, since we have so great a cloud of witnesses surrounding us . . . (12:1a)[2]

The Christian life is not a game of hopscotch. It is a hard-fought, tough-minded race.[3] The word translated "race" is from the Greek term *agōna,* from which we get the word *agony.* The writer is picturing athletes in an agonizing footrace, running for the finish line, cheered on by the faithful example of the heroes of faith from past generations.

Analysis of the Agony

All believers have been placed in life's arena to participate in the race of faith. In verses 1b–3, the writer coaches us on how to get ready for the race and how to stay on track.

Preparation for the Race

As we limber up before taking our places at the starting blocks, the writer advises us:

> Let us also lay aside every encumbrance, and the sin which so easily entangles us, and let us run with endurance the race that is set before us. (v. 1b)

The first thing the writer tells us to lay aside is anything and everything that might weigh us down and keep us from running well. An "encumbrance" is any excess weight. The Greek term from which we get this word literally means "mass" or "bulk." For a runner, this might be a bulky set of sweatpants. For a Christian, it's anything that slows the pace in the progress of our faith: an indifferent attitude, a lack of mental discipline, procrastination, impatience, or a motley wardrobe of other things that should be boxed up and thrown away.

The second bit of advice is to shed the "sin which so easily entangles us." What is this sin? The context of Hebrews 10, 11, and 12 suggests it is the sin of unbelief. This particular sin affects us like a cramp in the leg, causing us to break our stride or hobble off the track altogether.

2. The *therefore* of Hebrews 12:1 ties chapter 12 to chapter 11 in a cause-and-effect relationship. Consequently, the "cloud of witnesses surrounding us" refers to those in chapter 11, whose lives were such an eloquent testimony of faith.

3. For other athletic metaphors, see 1 Corinthians 9:24–27, Galatians 2:2, Philippians 2:16, 1 Timothy 6:12, 2 Timothy 2:5.

Command to Runners

The writer goes on to tell us to "run with endurance the race that is set before us." The term *endurance* means "to abide under" or "to wait with patience" (also used in 10:36). William Barclay comments on the word as follows:

> The word is *hupomonē* which does not mean the patience which sits down and accepts things but the patience which masters them. It is not some romantic thing which lends us wings to fly over the difficulties and the hard places. It is a determination, unhurrying and yet undelaying, which goes steadily on and refuses to be deflected. Obstacles do not daunt it and discouragements do not take its hope away. It is the steadfast endurance which carries on until in the end it gets there.[4]

Technique for Running

In verse 2 the writer examines our stride and instructs us to keep our head up, while

> fixing our eyes on Jesus, the author and perfecter of faith, who for the joy set before Him endured the cross, despising the shame, and has sat down at the right hand of the throne of God.

The first word in this verse is from the verb *aphoraō*. It means "to look away from all else and fix one's gaze upon."[5] Greek scholar Brooke Foss Westcott comments on this present participle, suggesting that it means attention focused "not only at the first moment, but constantly during the whole struggle."[6]

And who is the one upon which we are to have this intense, continual focus? Jesus, the *author* and *perfecter* of faith, the one who both started and finished the race.

As runners, our eyes must be trained on Him. We shouldn't turn our heads back to see where the other runners are, and we shouldn't get distracted by things on the sidelines. We should instead look to

4. William Barclay, *The Letter to the Hebrews*, rev. ed., The Daily Study Bible Series (Philadelphia, Pa.: Westminster Press, 1976), p. 173.

5. For a good example of what is meant here, see Acts 7:55–56, which describes Stephen in his hour of martyrdom.

6. Brooke Foss Westcott, *The Epistle to the Hebrews* (reprint, Grand Rapids, Mich.: William B. Eerdmans Publishing Co., 1973), pp. 394–95.

Him, for He ran the race with endurance and triumphed. He endured the Cross, suffered the shame, but at the last crossed the finish line to sit down at the right hand of God the Father.

And what kind of person is this Jesus to whom we are to run? An experienced runner Himself. A runner with perfect form. But most of all, one who is compassionate and sympathetic to our stumblings (4:15).

Attitude While Running

A positive mental attitude is important if a runner is to hang tough and fight off the fatigue and frustration of the race. Such an attitude is encouraged in verse 3.

> For consider Him who has endured such hostility by sinners against Himself, so that you may not grow weary and lose heart.

Consider means "to reckon, compare, weigh, think over." The salient point is that we are to so fix our eyes on Jesus that our minds block out any distractions. As we meditate on the grueling race He ran, with all its catcalls from the carping crowd, we can't help but get a burst of adrenaline for the faltering legs of our faith.

Applications to Keep Us from Quitting

Faith is not some warm flush of feeling that comes over us when our favorite hymns are piped through the church organ. Faith is a mind-set, a determined plan to finish the race God has set before us—regardless of our handicaps, the condition of the track, the obstacles in our path, or how inclement the weather is on any given day of the race.

Here are a couple of applications to keep us on the inside track to pleasing God.

First: *Claim the grace to persevere.* When the wind is in your face, when your legs wobble beneath you, when the crowd boos your efforts, call to God for the grace of a second wind.

> He gives strength to the weary,
> And to him who lacks might He increases power.
> Though youths grow weary and tired,
> And vigorous young men stumble badly,
> Yet those who wait for the Lord
> Will gain new strength;
> They will mount up with wings like eagles,

They will walk and not become weary.
(Isa. 40:29–31)

Second: *Remember you are never alone.* Nothing will dampen your spirits and cut your stride like the feeling that you're all alone and that nobody has ever run this race before. Our strength is renewed when we realize we're not alone—that the way has been trodden by the feet of generations of faithful believers.

> I thank Thee that this Christian way whereon I walk is no untried or uncharted road, but a road beaten hard by the footsteps of saints, apostles, prophets, and martyrs.[7]

And, most importantly, it has been trodden by the Lord Jesus Himself—the author and perfecter of faith.

Living Insights STUDY ONE

The dominant theme of Hebrews 12 is that of a race. The apostle Paul also develops this theme in 1 Corinthians and 2 Timothy. Let's combine these sections of Scripture to learn all we can about running.

- Read the following passages; then write down your observations about the race every Christian must run.

The Race

1 Corinthians 9:24–27 ______________________________

____

____

2 Timothy 2:5 __________________________________

____

____

Hebrews 12:1–3 ________________________________

____

____

7. John Baillie, A *Diary of Private Prayer* (New York, N.Y.: Charles Scribner's Sons, 1977), p. 25.

Living Insights

When it comes to the race of faith, are you breezing along with the wind at your back, or are you limping to the sidelines with a charley-horsed calf and a stitch in your side?

If you feel more like giving up than pressing on, don't lose hope. With every painful step, your muscles of faith are becoming lean and strong—and with every wheezing breath, you're drawing closer to the finish line. But for a cool splash of water to refresh you on your way and keep you from quitting, let's personalize those last two applications.

- *Claim the grace to persevere.* Just when you think you can't move another inch, God will blow a gentle breath to give you a second wind. That breath may come through a detour past a gurgling brook, an afternoon's rest in a friend's backyard hammock, or a quiet evening with the Lord and His Word. What best rejuvenates you? Schedule some time this week to let God refresh your spirit.

- *Remember you are never alone.* Of course, the Lord is always with you, running with you every step of the way. But He's also provided some tangible encouragement in the form of others who have shared your experiences. What are some ways you could draw from these resources of empathy?

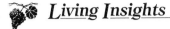

Chapter 10

Flip Side of Love

Hebrews 12:4–13

In his chapter "Praise God for the Furnace," A. W. Tozer writes:

> It was the enraptured Rutherford who could shout in the midst of serious and painful trials, "Praise God for the hammer, the file, and the furnace."
>
> The hammer is a useful tool, but the nail, if it had feeling and intelligence, could present another side of the story. For the nail knows the hammer only as an opponent, a brutal, merciless enemy who lives to pound it into submission, to beat it down out of sight and clinch it into place. That is the nail's view of the hammer, and it is accurate except for one thing: The nail forgets that both it and the hammer are servants of the same workman. Let the nail but remember that the hammer is held by the workman and all resentment toward it will disappear. The carpenter decides whose head shall be beaten next and what hammer shall be used in the beating. That is his sovereign right. When the nail has surrendered to the will of the workman and has gotten a little glimpse of his benign plans for its future it will yield to the hammer without complaint.
>
> The file is more painful still, for its business is to bite into the soft metal, scraping and eating away the edges till it has shaped the metal to its will. Yet the file has, in truth, no real will in the matter, but serves another master as the metal also does. It is the master and not the file that decides how much shall be eaten away, what shape the metal shall take, and how long the painful filing shall continue. Let the metal accept the will of the master and it will not try to dictate when or how it shall be filed.
>
> As for the furnace, it is the worst of all. Ruthless and savage, it leaps at every combustible thing that enters it and never relaxes its fury till it has reduced it all to shapeless ashes. All that refuses to burn is melted to a mass of helpless matter, without will or purpose of its own. When everything is melted that

> will melt and all is burned that will burn, then and not till then the furnace calms down and rests from its destructive fury.[1]

How could anyone praise God for the hammer, the file, and the furnace? Because of love for the hand that wields the hammer, works the file, and stokes the furnace—the loving hand of our heavenly Father.

Our Greatest Need: Confident Endurance

Some have argued that maximum love makes discipline unnecessary. Yet the Solomonic wisdom of Proverbs diametrically opposes that line of reasoning.

> He who spares his rod hates his son,
> But he who loves him disciplines him diligently.
> (13:24)

The truth of the matter is that children long for boundaries. They give them a sense of security, a feeling that they are watched over and cared for, as Psalm 23 indicates: "Thy rod and Thy staff, they *comfort* me" (v. 4b, emphasis added).

Faithful, mature parents recognize this truth by setting—and enforcing—boundaries. That is the flip side of love, and that is what Hebrews 12:4–13 is all about.

We not only need confident assurance that we are loved and watched over, we also need confident *endurance.* That is a major chord in the writer's symphonic development of Hebrews. That fact is stated in 10:35–36, exemplified in chapter 11, and encouraged in 12:1–3.

One of the best ways to endure is to consider the hostility Christ endured at the hands of sinners (v. 3). A look back to 5:8 reminds us that "although He was a Son, He learned obedience from the things which He suffered." Every royal privilege was laid aside when this prince became a pauper and left His throne in heaven to become one of us.

Enduring the Father's Discipline

If Jesus, God's perfect Son, endured suffering to learn obedience, how much more should we expect to go through the same curriculum.

1. A. W. Tozer, *The Root of the Righteous* (Camp Hill, Pa.: Christian Publications, 1986), pp. 134–36.

Before presenting several principles to help sufferers endure hurt, the writer lays down a couple of basic absolutes.

Discipline Is Better Than Death

> You have not yet resisted to the point of shedding blood in your striving against sin. (12:4)

The Greek term translated "striving" is *antagōnizomai.* From it we get our word *antagonism.* It refers to suffering brought about by external persecution, sinful things done against believers to terrorize them into abandoning the faith.

When the Lord's discipline is seen against the backdrop of the world's persecution, it appears light indeed. For however painful, it is purposeful, aimed at transforming our character—not destroying it. Consequently, discipline at the hands of the Lord is preferable to death at the hands of the world.

Discipline Proves the Father's Love

> And you have forgotten the exhortation which is addressed to you as sons,
> "My Son, do not regard lightly the discipline
> of the Lord,
> Nor faint when you are reproved by Him;
> For those whom the Lord loves He
> disciplines,
> And He scourges every son whom He
> receives."
> (vv. 5–6)

The writer uses this passage from Proverbs 3:11–12 to identify two reactions to God's discipline. The first is to attach little importance to His discipline. The second reaction is to cave in or lose heart and grow weak in our faith (compare v. 3b).

To avoid these two extremes, we need to place suffering in its proper context, remembering that it is a means by which God communicates with us. As C. S. Lewis put it, "God whispers to us in our pleasures, speaks in our conscience, but shouts in our pains: it is His megaphone to rouse a deaf world."[2]

This is where faith comes in. To endure, we have to trust that God's discipline is motivated by love and His use of pain is to reassure us that we are indeed His children.

2. C. S. Lewis, *The Problem of Pain* (New York, N.Y.: Macmillan Publishing Co., 1962), p. 93.

Four Basic Principles That Help Amidst Hurt

Hebrews 12:7–11 provides some rudimentary principles to put a little salve on the switch marks endured behind God's woodshed.

Discipline Assures Us of Sonship

> It is for discipline that you endure; God deals with you as with sons; for what son is there whom his father does not discipline? But if you are without discipline, of which all have become partakers, then you are illegitimate children and not sons. (vv. 7–8)

God's classroom course on raising His children includes pain in its curriculum. This discipline is the highest compliment He pays us, because it assures us that we are His legitimate children. If we were illegitimate, He wouldn't take the trouble. Therefore, we should strive to endure the discipline that will conform our character to His.

However, many would rather have a benevolent grandfather in heaven whose prime interest is our contentment, than have a Father whose prime interest is our character.[3]

Discipline Deepens and Enhances Life

> Furthermore, we had earthly fathers to discipline us, and we respected them; shall we not much rather be subject to the Father of spirits, and live? (v. 9)

Verse 9 introduces an argument from the lesser to the greater. If we submit to our earthly fathers, how much more should we submit to our heavenly Father. Life is the by-product of submitting to God. When we stay on the straight and narrow path of obedience, our life is enhanced and enriched (see Prov. 6:23, 10:16–17, 29:15a).

This is why Aleksandr Solzhenitsyn could say:

> It was only when I lay there on rotting prison straw that I sensed within myself the first stirrings of good. Gradually, it was disclosed to me that the line separating good and evil passes, not through states, nor between classes, nor between political parties either, but right through every human heart, and through all human hearts. So, bless you, prison, for having been in my life.[4]

3. Lewis, *The Problem of Pain,* pp. 40–41.

4. Aleksandr Solzhenitsyn, *The Gulag Archipelago,* as quoted by Philip Yancey in *Where Is God When It Hurts?* (Grand Rapids, Mich.: Zondervan Publishing House, 1977), p. 51.

Discipline Continues for Our Benefit

> For they disciplined us for a short time as seemed best to them, but He disciplines us for our good, that we may share His holiness. (Heb. 12:10)

Our earthly fathers were human, fallible, sometimes inconsistent, sometimes unfair, and sometimes even extreme. Yet they disciplined us "as seemed best to them." God, however, is perfect, infallible, consistent, fair, and always uses appropriate discipline to fit the offense. And His training doesn't end when we're eighteen or twenty-one or out of the house and on our own. His training lasts all our lives, even into our senior years. Why? That we might share His holiness. He chisels away on our character like Michelangelo did on his famous sculpture *David.* And He doesn't lay down the chisel until the work is complete.

Romans 8:28 tells us the divine motivation of the sculptor.

> And we know that God causes all things to work together for good to those who love God, to those who are called according to His purpose.

But verse 29 gives us the image in the divine mind of the sculptor.

> For whom He foreknew, He also predestined to become conformed to the image of His Son, that He might be the first-born among many brethren.

Discipline, Though Initially Painful, Is Ultimately Valuable

> All discipline for the moment seems not to be joyful, but sorrowful; yet to those who have been trained by it, afterwards it yields the peaceful fruit of righteousness. (Heb. 12:11)

The discipline of God is like pruning shears in the hands of the gardener. Although the process of pruning is painful for the plant, it is ultimately productive—both on a physical and on a spiritual level.

> "I am the true vine, and My Father is the vinedresser. Every branch in Me that does not bear fruit, He takes away; and every branch that bears fruit, He prunes it, that it may bear more fruit." (John 15:1–2)

The Ultimate Goal: Inner Healing

Discipline produces *security* by assuring us of our sonship; *maturity* by deepening and enhancing our life; *conformity* by continuing throughout life for our benefit; and *spirituality* by pruning us for fruitfulness.

The ultimate goal of discipline, however, is our inner healing.

> Therefore, strengthen the hands that are weak and the knees that are feeble, and make straight paths for your feet, so that the limb which is lame may not be put out of joint, but rather be healed. (Heb. 12:12–13)

Discipline is not something we should fight or resist or run from. Rather, it is something we should brace ourselves for, because our suffering is but a means to a greater end—to make us spiritually healthy and whole so we can run the race set before us with endurance.

Since we're all interconnected members of one body, we should strive not only to care for ourselves but also to care for the needs of others within the body. Especially when they are suffering (Gal. 6:1–2, Eph. 4:15–16, 1 Thess. 5:14, Heb. 13:3).

The reason we should take such care of the body is because it is God's *magnum opus,* His masterpiece that mirrors the very image of Christ. And it is because we are His "great work" that God takes such meticulous care in the formation of our character. As C. S. Lewis wrote:

> We are, not metaphorically but in very truth, a Divine work of art, something that God is making, and therefore something with which He will not be satisfied until it has a certain character. Here again we come up against what I have called the "intolerable compliment." Over a sketch made idly to amuse a child, an artist may not take much trouble: he may be content to let it go even though it is not exactly as he meant it to be. But over the great picture of his life—the work which he loves, though in a different fashion, as intensely as a man loves a woman or a mother a child—he will take endless trouble—and would, doubtless, thereby *give* endless trouble to the picture if it were sentient. One can imagine a sentient picture, after being rubbed and scraped and re-commenced for the tenth time, wishing that it were only a thumb-nail sketch whose making was over in a minute. In the same way, it is natural for us to wish that God had designed for us a less glorious and less arduous destiny; but then we are wishing not for more love but for less.[5]

5. Lewis, *The Problem of Pain,* pp. 42–43.

Living Insights STUDY ONE

Hebrews 12 develops four principles that can help us in the midst of hurt. If you do a careful search, you will see that all four of these principles are actually fully developed themes which run through all of Scripture.

- Let's look for these themes. Using a Bible concordance to help identify passages that develop these topics, list the references in the following charts; then jot down a summary of each passage.

Helping the Hurting

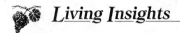

Security	
References	Summaries

Maturity	
References	Summaries

Conformity	
References	Summaries

Spirituality	
References	Summaries

Living Insights STUDY TWO

The discipline our earthly fathers gave us was preparatory to the discipline of our heavenly Father. At the time, the discipline of both fathers was painful. But in retrospect there was much we learned from the discipline that we can be thankful for.

- Write your father a letter. You may choose your earthly father or your heavenly Father. Write the letter on the subject of discipline, talking about how you responded to his reproof at different times in your life. Perhaps you can honestly include a paragraph of gratitude. If you choose to write to your Father in heaven, use this as a time of prayer.

Chapter 11

WATCH OUT FOR WORLDLINESS!

Hebrews 12:14–17

There is more nonsense per square inch about *worldliness* than perhaps any other subject in the Christian life. Usually, worldliness is reduced to a laundry list of taboos—the nasty nine, the terrible ten, or the dirty dozen, depending on whose list you go by.

The dos and don'ts sound like they come straight from Sinai, but the truth of the matter is, they originate from our own parochial prejudices.

We want to watch out for worldliness, but we also want to watch out for the legalistic labels that some condescending Christians stick on many areas of life where God has granted us freedom.

The key to an abundant life under the lordship of Christ is not trying to impress Him with the check marks on our laundry list but trying to live like He lived—full of grace and truth, not full of legalism and pious platitudes.

A Brief Analysis of Worldliness

Sometimes finding out what something *isn't* can help us discern what it actually *is*. With that in mind, let's look at three things worldliness is not.

First: *Worldliness isn't something external.* It's possible to have a tawdry dust jacket on a Pulitzer Prize-winning novel. It's also possible to have an aesthetically pleasing cover on some hackneyed piece of pulp. Just as you can't judge a book by its cover, so you can't judge a person's relationship with Christ by externals.

Second: *Worldliness isn't based on preference, tradition, or feelings.* Some people prefer an organ in church; others prefer no accompaniment at all. Which is more spiritual? Which is more accepted in God's eyes? Neither. They're simply a matter of preference, tradition, or feelings. What pleases God is the *heart* that overflows in praise, not the instrument through which it finds expression (compare Mark 7:6 with Eph. 5:18–19).

Third: *Worldliness isn't something geographical or variable.* If it's worldly in New York City, it's worldly in Dime Box, Texas. Worldliness is not dictated by the undulating caprice of cultural standards; it's dictated by the Word of God.

What, then, is worldliness? Essentially, it's *a mentality that discounts and denies Christ as Lord.* First John 2:15–16 implies that the essence of worldliness is an attitude of the heart.

> Do not love the world, nor the things in the world. If anyone loves the world, the love of the Father is not in him. For all that is in the world, the lust of the flesh and the lust of the eyes and the boastful pride of life, is not from the Father, but is from the world.

Although worldliness originates in the heart, its ultimate enticement comes from Satan.

> We know that we are of God, and the whole world lies in the power of the evil one. (5:19)

Like the ubiquitous brown smog that envelops the Los Angeles basin, worldliness is everywhere. We can't inhale without taking a breath of some carcinogenic vapors that are foreign to the fresh-air values of God's kingdom. Worldliness is dangerous because of its infiltrating influence. It goes into our lungs, through our bloodstream, and eventually winds up in our brain. And that destroys the way we think, affecting the decisions we make. That's why worldliness is so dangerous. It's a slow and subtle process of spiritual suffocation.

The Godliness-Worldliness Conflict

Hebrews 12 is not primarily a chapter on worldliness; it's a chapter about running a race. Verse 1 exhorts us to run with endurance. Verse 2 instructs us to fix our eyes on Jesus while we're running. Verse 3 urges us to focus our thoughts on the race Jesus ran so that we won't grow weary in ours. Verses 4–11 alert us to the training program God uses to keep us up and running. Verses 12–13 inspire us to get healthy and get back in the race. Finally, verses 14–17 form something of a rest stop for runners to catch their breath and get their bearings. Because there's something ahead that could throw us off track—and that something is worldliness.

In these last four verses there are two positive commands and three negative warnings.

Two Positive Commands

The positive commands grow out of verse 14.

> Pursue peace with all men, and the sanctification without which no one will see the Lord.

The writer coaches those wanting to run the race of faith to *pursue peace with all people* and to *pursue being different.* Regarding the pursuit of peace, the world system says it's a dog-eat-dog world and the puppies don't make it. God's system says, "If possible, so far as it depends on you, be at peace with all men" (Rom. 12:18). The world system says bite back and claw your way to the top. God's system says turn the other cheek and let whoever wishes to be great among you be your servant (Matt. 5:39, 20:26).

Regarding the pursuit of a godly standard, the world system says to conform to its own carnal ideas. God's system, however, tells us to be transformed (Rom. 12:2). The word the writer of Hebrews uses is *sanctification.* The term carries with it the ideas of separation and difference. When we are morally *separate* from the values of the world, and when we operate by means that are *different* from theirs, we will stand out from them like daylight from darkness (see Matt. 5:1–16, Phil. 2:14–15).

Three Negative Warnings

The negative warnings are found in Hebrews 12:15–16.

> See to it that no one comes short of the grace of God; that no root of bitterness springing up causes trouble, and by it many be defiled; that there be no immoral or godless person like Esau, who sold his own birthright for a single meal.

The first warning is: *Don't let anyone come short of grace.* When we live by the rigid requirements of the Law, we fall short of God's best for our lives. God's best is a supple life characterized by grace. It is a life that's free, ruled only by one law—the law of love, written not on hard, external tablets of stone but on the soft, inner linings of our hearts (Jer. 31:33, Rom. 14:15, 1 Cor. 13, 2 Cor. 5:14a, Eph. 5:2). Grace is the green pasture where God wants His sheep to graze—not the narrow, fenced-off holding pens of the Law.

The second warning is: *Don't allow bitterness to take root.*[1] The picture is one of a tenacious root, stubbornly clinging to the soil of

1. This warning comes from Deuteronomy 29:14–21.

worldliness. When bitterness burrows underneath the surface of a person's life, it slowly develops an intricate network of roots that anchors it to the soil. Once bitterness sprouts to the surface, it soon bears its poisonous fruit. When we first see its upshoots, we should immediately unearth the soil around it and root it up (Eph. 4:26–27, 31). If we're not diligent about this, it will be just a matter of time before our lives and our churches are completely overgrown (Prov. 24:30–34).

The third warning is: *Don't tolerate the Esau syndrome.* Esau is a perfect illustration of a worldly person—one who values material realities over spiritual ones, one who lives by sight rather than by faith, one who lives for today rather than for eternity. Esau had come home from his hunting trip, empty-handed and famished. So famished was he that he traded the spiritual blessing of his birthright for a measly bowl of vegetable stew (Gen. 25:27–34). No doubt, his immorality and godlessness stemmed from the low value he placed on spiritual things, which amounted to the paltry sum of a hot meal.

Esau's choice led to some serious consequences, as Hebrews 12:17 reveals.

> For you know that even afterwards, when he desired to inherit the blessing, he was rejected, for he found no place for repentance, though he sought for it with tears.

At a later time Esau, with a full stomach and full control of his faculties, realized how foolish he had been. He pleaded for a reversal of his fate, pleaded with tears, but the text is brutally final: "he was rejected, for he found no place for repentance."

In his case the cost of worldly thinking sent him spiraling into spiritual bankruptcy. And no amount of repentance bought him a reversal of the fate he had bartered for himself.

Resisting a Worldly Mentality

Now, let's take worldliness out of the theoretical realm and into the practical. How can we resist a worldly mentality? First: *Adjust your pace after starting the race.* If you're in the race from here to eternity, you need to realize you're not running alone. You need to slow down to pat a fellow runner on the back. You need to stop now and then to pick up some exhausted runner who has fallen. You need to pursue peace, so that the members of the body of Christ are all running in step.

Second: *Imagine the consequences before you commit.* Realize before you jump into the race that it's a marathon, not a fifty-yard dash. The tendency is to shoot out of the starting blocks with a burst of speed, only to hyperventilate in the second lap. When that happens, it's easy to take a breather on the sidelines where worldliness is waiting to wrap a towel around you, rub your shoulders, and quench your thirst. That's why it's so important to fix our eyes on Jesus, our feet on the track, and our mind on finishing the race in championship form.

Living Insights STUDY ONE

The four verses we looked at in this study are rich in meaning and significance. We've listed a few key words from these verses for you to define. After you've discovered the definition, write a statement of significance for each one. It might help you to begin by looking at the context in which each term appears, then expand your view by looking at cross references, a dictionary, and perhaps even a Bible dictionary.

"Peace" (v. 14)

Definition:____

____

Significance:______________________________________

____

"Sanctification" (v. 14)

Definition:____

____

Significance:______________________________________

____

"Root" (v. 15)

Definition:____

____

Significance:______________________________________

____

"Bitterness" (v. 15)

Definition:______________________________

____

Significance:____________________________

____

"Birthright" (v. 16)

Definition:______________________________

____

Significance:____________________________

____

"Blessing" (v. 17)

Definition:______________________________

____

Significance:____________________________

____

"Repentance" (v. 17)

Definition:______________________________

____

Significance:____________________________

____

Living Insights — STUDY TWO

We have defined worldliness as *a mentality which discounts or denies Christ as Lord.* Let's use today's Living Insights to probe deeper into this subject.

- Would you agree with the definition of worldliness presented in our lesson?

____

____

- How was worldliness defined when you were growing up?

____

____

____

- How does worldliness relate to externals? How about internals?

____

____

____

- What is the relationship between worldliness and preference?

____

____

____

- We learned that worldliness isn't geographical. Would you agree or disagree? Why?

____

____

- How does worldliness tie into bitterness?

____

____

____

- Have you tolerated an "Esau syndrome" in your life in recent days? If so, what do you think you should do about it?

____

____

____

Chapter 12

OUR AWESOME, CONSUMING GOD

Hebrews 12:18–29

In a chapter on methods of exposition, the book *Modern Rhetoric* describes the nature of comparison and contrast.

> It is natural for us, in confronting an unfamiliar object, to set it against the familiar. We instinctively want to know in what ways it is like the familiar and in what ways different. This is a simple, and essential, way of sorting out our experience of the world.
>
> A child asks, "What is a zebra?" We reply, "Oh, a zebra—it's an animal sort of like a mule, but it's not as big as a mule. And it has stripes like a tiger, black and white stripes all over. But you remember that a tiger's stripes are black and orange." Here we have used both comparison and contrast. We have compared the shape of the zebra to that of the mule, but have contrasted the two animals in size. And we have compared the stripes of the zebra to the stripes of a tiger, but have contrasted them in color. If the child knows what mules and tigers are like, he now has a pretty good idea of a zebra.[1]

In a similar way the writer of Hebrews compares and contrasts the Old Covenant with the New, using the representative images of Mount Sinai and Mount Zion.

A Brief Review

Our passage today explodes on the canvas like an impressionist painting, bursting with wild, untamed images: a foreboding mountain, a blaze of flames, a whirlwind, a consuming fire. The natural tendency, especially for children walking through an art gallery, would be to recoil at a picture like this.

We know, however, from the broader context of Hebrews, that the writer's intent is to get us to do just the opposite. He wants us

1. Cleanth Brooks and Robert Penn Warren, *Modern Rhetoric*, 3d ed. (New York, N.Y.: Harcourt, Brace and World, 1970), pp. 69–70.

to draw near, not pull away. In doing so, he has pictured Christ as the bridge that spans the abyss between a holy God and His errant creation. Jesus is the mediator, the high priest who guarantees us access to God (9:11–15). Because of that, we are exhorted not only to draw near, but to do so with confidence (4:16).

But if all that is true, where do the ominous images of Mount Sinai fit in?

A Strong Contrast

The writer leads us down a path that passes by two mountains. The first is Mount Sinai, where Moses received the stone tablets of the Law.

> For you have not come to a mountain that may be touched and to a blazing fire, and to darkness and gloom and whirlwind, and to the blast of a trumpet and the sound of words which sound was such that those who heard begged that no further word should be spoken to them. For they could not bear the command, "If even a beast touches the mountain, it will be stoned." And so terrible was the sight, that Moses said, "I am full of fear and trembling." (12:18–21)

The writer uses Mount Sinai to represent the Law and all its requirements. Like a painter with his skillful brush, he brings to life all the old emotions that accompanied the Old Covenant: the fear, the trembling, the awe. For a fuller description, compare the accounts in Exodus 19:12–13, 17–18, 21–22, and Deuteronomy 5:23–26.

Even centuries later, the readers felt the tremors from the quaking of Mount Sinai. They heard the deafening echo of the Almighty's thunderous voice. They felt the sheer terror shiver down their spines.

In resurrecting these old emotions, the writer seeks to steady—not scare—the runner. He seeks to encourage the runner by showing that the charted course doesn't pass by Sinai. It leads to another mountain altogether.

The writer now takes the runner's eyes off the mountain of stone in the distance, and turns them to the lush beauty of Mount Zion. And when he does, the runner's legs stop shaking and start to stabilize.

> But you have come to Mount Zion and to the city of the living God, the heavenly Jerusalem, and to myriads of angels, to the general assembly and church of the first-born who are enrolled in heaven, and to God,

> the Judge of all, and to the spirits of righteous men made perfect, and to Jesus, the mediator of a new covenant, and to the sprinkled blood, which speaks better than the blood of Abel. (Heb. 12:22–24)

This scenic mountain symbolizes the presence of the Almighty. It is a landscape terraced with the hierarchies of heaven, verdant with affection and affirmation, and redolent with righteousness.

There we stand face-to-face with "the Judge of all." But we don't need to stand with our knees knocking and our teeth chattering. We don't stand cringing; we stand confident. Why? Because we are recipients of a new covenant, ratified by the blood of Jesus. The new arrangement is not one of "Thou shalts" and "Thou shalt nots." It's a mountain of grace we can all come to and circle around.

A Final Warning

The New Covenant is far better than the Old Covenant. But it is also far more vulnerable to being abused. When running by grace, we sometimes tend to shorten our strides and cut a few corners as we round the turn in the track. It's easy to slack off a bit, towel off the sweat, and slow down to a comfortable trot.

That's why verses 25–29 were written. They function like a megaphoned warning from our Coach.

> See to it that you do not refuse Him who is speaking. For if those did not escape when they refused him who warned them on earth, much less shall we escape who turn away from Him who warns from heaven. And His voice shook the earth then, but now He has promised, saying, "Yet once more I will shake not only the earth, but also the heaven." And this expression, "Yet once more," denotes the removing of those things which can be shaken, as of created things, in order that those things which cannot be shaken may remain. Therefore, since we receive a kingdom which cannot be shaken, let us show gratitude, by which we may offer to God an acceptable service with reverence and awe; for our God is a consuming fire.

Two warnings radiate from the megaphone, one negative, one positive.

Negatively, verse 25 tells us: *"Don't refuse Him who is speaking!"* Just because there is a new arrangement doesn't mean there has been a change in management. Just because parents, for example, change the rules of the household as their children grow older and more responsible doesn't mean the children's respect for the parents should change. In fact, the respect should increase as the children mature and gain greater understanding of the character of their parents.

The same is true for the children of the New Covenant. The Word we have from God should be even more revered, as it comes not from an earthly mountain but from the pinnacle of heaven. Also, the display of power on Mount Sinai was limited. Mount Zion's display, however, will shake not only the earth but also the heavens.

Therefore, logic would argue, if His Word was to be obeyed then, how much more should it be obeyed now.

Positively, verse 28 tells us: *"Let us show gratitude."* The word *gratitude* is from the Greek term *charis,* meaning "grace." Other translations of the phrase could be "Let us hold on to grace" or "Let us keep on recognizing grace." The gist of verse 28 is: Since by grace we have received a permanent relationship with God and a kingdom that cannot be shaken, we should keep clinging to grace so that we can approach Him the way He deserves to be approached—with reverence and awe.

When we come confidently to the throne of grace but not with reverence and awe, we fall short of the course grace would have us run, tripping on the very steps to that throne.

The God enthroned for the administration of the New Covenant is still the same God who sat there during the administration of the Old. He hasn't changed. He is still a consuming fire (v. 29, from Deut. 4:24).

Some Personal Questions

A God of grace can be easily taken advantage of. But when we abuse that relationship, something in us is diminished. Something sacred dies—the fear of God. When we treat holy things casually, when we stop taking our shoes off before the burning bush, it is we who change—not the bush.

Are you taking the God of grace for granted? Do you talk flippantly about Him? Do you worship Him with casual indifference? Do you regard His Word lightly? Do you live a cavalier life of abusing grace?

Don't fall short of the grace of God, my friend. Please. He has been too gracious for us to take Him for granted. He has been too faithful for us to falter on the very steps to His throne.

Living Insights STUDY ONE

Hebrews 12 describes the race we're in as a *grace race.* This distinction is made clear by the contrasting of two mountains: Sinai and Zion.

- There is a similar contrast drawn in Galatians 4:21–31. In these verses, Hagar and Sarah are contrasted, along with the same two mountains. Using these two passages (Gal. 4:21–31 and Heb. 12:18–24), list the contrasts between grace and law.

Contrasting Grace and Law

Verse	Grace Principles

Verse	Law Principles

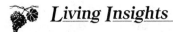

Living Insights STUDY TWO

This study concluded with some very probing questions. What went through your mind when you thought about how they applied to you?

- Use this time to set up a visit with another person. It could be for lunch, dinner, dessert, coffee . . . golfing, jogging, walking . . . whatever. The purpose of this visit is to ask one another the question, How significant is God to you? Provide yourselves adequate time to answer the question thoroughly. After talking it over with your friend, why not talk to God about it too. Ask Him to keep you from ever abusing His wonderful grace.

Chapter 13

BROTHERS, STRANGERS, AND PRISONERS

Hebrews 13:1–3

Charles W. Colson, special counsel to former President Nixon and convicted Watergate conspirator, served a prison sentence that changed the course of his life. Emerging from his incarceration with a strong faith and a heightened awareness of the needs of prisoners, Colson founded Prison Fellowship. Here is a moving story of his visit to an Indiana penitentiary.

> My schedule was extremely tight, so after we finished "Amazing Grace" we said our good-byes and began filing out. We were crowded into the caged area between the two massive gates when we noticed one volunteer had stayed back and was with James Brewer in his cell. I went to get the man because the warden could not operate the gates until we had all cleared out.
>
> "I'm sorry, we have to leave," I said, looking nervously at my watch, knowing a plane stood waiting at a nearby airstrip to fly me to Indianapolis to meet with Governor Orr. . . .
>
> "Oh, yes," the volunteer looked up. "Give us just a minute, please. This is important," he added softly.
>
> "No, I'm sorry," I snapped. "I can't keep the governor waiting. We must go."
>
> "I understand," the man said, still speaking softly, "but this is important. You see, I'm Judge Clement. I'm the man who sentenced James here to die. But now he's my brother and we want a minute to pray together."
>
> I stood frozen in the cell doorway. It didn't matter who I kept waiting. . . . Anywhere other than the kingdom of God, that inmate might have killed that judge with his bare hands—or wanted to anyway. Now they were one, their faces reflecting an indescribable expression of love as they prayed together.
>
> Though he could hardly speak, on the way out of the prison Judge Clement told me he had been praying

for Brewer every day since he had sentenced him four years earlier. . . .

Taking the gospel to people wherever they are—death row, the ghetto, or next door—*is frontline evangelism.* Frontline love.[1]

Today's passage in Hebrews encourages us to "remember the prisoners, as though in prison with them" (v. 3). Let's take a closer look at this "frontline love" that welcomes the stranger, befriends the friendless, and loves the unlovely.

Wrapping Up a Lengthy Letter

Hebrews 13 is a catchall kind of conclusion into which all of the writer's closing comments are thrown. Up till now the writer has focused on our vertical relationship with God. But in chapter 13 he shifts to our horizontal relationships with others. Prior to this chapter the discussions have been lengthy, with elaborate digressions. Now, however, the discussions are terse and to the point. Before chapter 13 the content has been more theological. In this chapter, though, the warnings are personal and the commands practical.

With this general overview of the letter, let's turn our focus to the specifics of chapter 13.

Verse 1 addresses our relationship with other Christians. Verse 2 turns our attention to our relationship with strangers. Verse 3 shifts to our responsibilities to prisoners. Verse 4 gives advice regarding the marriage relationship. Verses 5–6 talk about our relationship to money. Verses 7 and 17 deal with our relationship to those in positions of spiritual leadership. Verse 8 makes a doctrinal statement on the person of Christ. Verse 9 warns us regarding our relationship to strange doctrine. Verses 10–14 are a digression on animal sacrifices that applies to our relationship with Christ. Verses 15–16 touch on our relationship to God and the type of sacrifices that please Him. Verses 18–19 are a personal prayer request from the writer. And finally, verses 20–25 form a closing benediction to the letter.

As you can see, there is no logical flow to chapter 13. Rather, it is more like a literary collage, comprised of snippets of last-minute instructions and practical advice.

1. Charles W. Colson, *Loving God* (Grand Rapids, Mich.: Zondervan Publishing House, Judith Markham Books, 1983), pp. 193–94.

Giving Thought to Three Areas of Need

Verses 1–3 come at us like jabs from a boxer. But although they come quickly, they carry a lot of punch. Each verse makes a forceful impact upon our responsibilities in our relationships with others.

To Christians

> Let love of the brethren continue. (v. 1)

The Greek word for "love" here is not the usual *agapē*, which is often used to describe divine love. It is *philadelphia*, which means "brotherly love." It's a compound of *philos*, another word for "love," and *adelphos*, the word for "brother."

There is a family warmth and heartfelt affection about the word *philos*. The verb form is best understood as "to cherish."

C. S. Lewis made an eloquent distinction between the love that lovers have for each other and this brotherly love which friends have.

> Lovers are always talking to one another about their love; Friends hardly ever about their Friendship. Lovers are normally face to face, absorbed in each other; Friends, side by side, absorbed in some common interest.[2]

For Christians, that common interest is Christ. And our relationship with Him automatically places us in a relationship with other believers. The letter to the Hebrews exhorts us to foster those friendships, because, as C. S. Lewis again noted, they don't come naturally to our culture.

> To the Ancients, Friendship seemed the happiest and most fully human of all loves; the crown of life and the school of virtue. The modern world, in comparison, ignores it. We admit of course that besides a wife and family a man needs a few "friends." But the very tone of the admission, and the sort of acquaintanceships which those who make it would describe as "friendships," show clearly that what they are talking about has very little to do with that *Philia* which Aristotle classified among the virtues or that *Amicitia* on which Cicero wrote a book. It is something quite marginal; not a main course in life's banquet; a diversion; something that fills up the chinks of one's time.[3]

2. C. S. Lewis, *The Four Loves* (New York, N.Y.: Harcourt Brace Jovanovich, 1960), p. 91.

3. Lewis, *The Four Loves*, pp. 87–88.

To Strangers

To prevent friendship from becoming provincial and ingrown, the writer shows that we are to open our door not only to saints but to strangers as well.

> Do not neglect to show hospitality to strangers, for by this some have entertained angels without knowing it. (v. 2)

The same word for "love" that is used in verse 1 is used in verse 2 in the compound *philoxenia,* meaning literally "love of strangers." In showing love to strangers we mirror God's love, which extends not only to those within His family but to those outside it (see Matt. 5:43–48).

By being hospitable to strangers, some have even entertained angels (compare Gen. 18:1–22 with 19:1). And none of us would like to close the door on that possibility.

But because of our American pioneer heritage, we have developed a pull-ourselves-up-by-the-bootstraps, God-helps-those-who-help-themselves philosophy about life—which tends to breed contempt rather than compassion for the down-and-out strangers in our society.

As Christians, however, we are not called to be jurors trying the case of the less fortunate; we are called to be Good Samaritans.

> "And all the nations will be gathered before Him; and He will separate them from one another, as the shepherd separates the sheep from the goats; and He will put the sheep on His right, and the goats on the left. Then the King will say to those on His right, 'Come, you who are blessed of My Father, inherit the kingdom prepared for you from the foundation of the world. For I was hungry, and you gave Me something to eat; I was thirsty, and you gave Me drink; I was a stranger, and you invited Me in; naked, and you clothed Me; I was sick, and you visited Me; I was in prison, and you came to Me.' Then the righteous will answer Him, saying, 'Lord, when did we see You hungry, and feed You, or thirsty, and give You drink? And when did we see You a stranger, and invite You in, or naked, and clothe You? And when did we see You sick, or in prison, and come to You?' And the King will answer and say to them, 'Truly I say to you, to the extent that you did it to one of these brothers of Mine, even the least of them, you did it to Me.'" (Matt. 25:32–40)

To Prisoners

The last phrase in verse 36—"I was in prison, and you came to Me"—introduces us to our third sphere of responsibility found in Hebrews 13.

> Remember the prisoners, as though in prison with them, and those who are ill-treated, since you yourselves also are in the body. (v. 3)

This verse addresses the needs of battered and broken believers who have been incarcerated—whether in penal institutions or in their own personal prisons. And we are to treat them the same way Christ would. We are to sympathize with their circumstances and alleviate their alienation by offering them our love.

The basis of our concern is that we are all members of the same body. When a thumb gets hit by a hammer, the whole body feels it. When a stomach gets a virus, the whole body aches.

> But now there are many members, but one body. And the eye cannot say to the hand, "I have no need of you"; or again the head to the feet, "I have no need of you" . . . that there should be no division in the body, but that the members should have the same care for one another. And if one member suffers, all the members suffer with it; if one member is honored, all the members rejoice with it. Now you are Christ's body, and individually members of it. (1 Cor. 12:20–21, 25–27)

Getting Practical by Getting Involved

Love is an up-close word. We really can't love at a distance. We have to get involved . . . roll up our sleeves . . . get our hands dirty. That's what the Good Samaritan did, remember (see Luke 10:29–37)?

Do you remember, too, that those who looked the other way and walked to the other side of the street were religious people (vv. 31–32)?

The writer to the Hebrews won't let us do that. He uses the first three verses of chapter 13 to turn our heads, to show us a world in need, and to impress upon us that we were put here to meet those needs by being the hands and feet of the Lord Jesus. That is how His love can come near. And that is how the world will recognize Him as Lord—when it sees Him in our lives.

Living Insights STUDY ONE

As opposed to the lengthy theological discussions developed in the first 12 chapters, chapter 13 is more economical in its style. Instead of a boatload of doctrine, it's more like a treasure chest full of one-carat gems of truth.

- Go through Hebrews 13 and make a list of all the topics that are covered in its twenty-five verses. Next, see if you can discover at least one other passage of Scripture that addresses each issue. Jot down the references in the right-hand column.

Overview of Hebrews 13	
Topics	Cross References

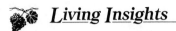

Living Insights

Today's lesson, with its three short, power-packed statements, brings to our attention three areas of need. Let's personalize each of these. In the space provided, write some specific applications. Then begin weaving them into the fabric of your life.

"Love . . . the Brethren"

"Show Hospitality to Strangers"

"Remember the Prisoners"

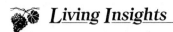

Chapter 14

COMMITMENT AND CONTENTMENT

(PART ONE)

Hebrews 13:4

In a *Time* magazine article titled "The Hollowing of America," John Leo reviewed Amitai Etzioni's book, *An Immodest Agenda: Rebuilding America Before the 21st Century.* In his review, he made special note of an alarming conclusion the author had come to regarding marriage.

> Etzioni's new book . . . sees the "ego-centered mentality" as the chief villain, rooted in American individualism but disastrously pushed along by the counterculture and self psychologies of Abraham Maslow and others. . . . He argues that attitudes unleashed since the '60s have so corroded American life that no political or economic renewal is possible unless those attitudes are changed.
>
> Etzioni cites Pollster Daniel Yankelovich, who found that 17% of Americans are deeply committed to a philosophy of self-fulfillment—a feeling that ego needs, sensation and excitement take priority over work and the needs of others, including spouse and children. Another 63%, whom Etzioni calls "the ambivalent majority," embrace the self-centered philosophy in varying degrees. "That they also hold on to old beliefs is important," he says, "but it does not belie the fact that 80% of Americans have been affected by the new mentality." . . .
>
> In the age of ego, marriage is often less an emotional bonding than a breakable alliance between self-seeking individuals.[1]

From this article it seems that the "hollowing of America" can be at least partially attributed to the rotting of the American family, the core of which is the marriage relationship. And once the core is destroyed, can the tree's fall be far behind?

1. John Leo, "The Hollowing of America," *Time*, December 20, 1982, p. 85.

Sizing Up the Scene: A Realistic Appraisal

The home is the basic unit of our society. And it's axiomatic that a nation is only as strong as its homes—enough weak homes add up to a weak nation.

The home was once an anvil upon which convictions were hammered out and character was forged. But for the past two or three decades it has taken a severe beating. It's been bashed on the talk shows and battered on the big screen.

The two wrecking balls that have pounded the home are *marital infidelity* and *material idolatry.* In Part One of this study we want to focus on *commitment* in marriage. In Part Two we will concentrate on *contentment* with material things.

Hearing God's Counsel: A Scriptural Analysis

There was a time when those committing adultery were branded with the letter A on their foreheads so their shame would be visible to all. Now, the sin is just as visible, but the shame has been erased. Sexual trysts and extramarital affairs are not only openly discussed on Oprah, Geraldo, and Donahue, they are almost evangelistically promoted as cures to marital boredom and a sundry of emotional deprivations.

But there is a law at work when wildly promiscuous oats are sown: The law of the harvest (see Gal. 6:7). Though there is pleasure in sin, it is only for a season (see Heb. 11:25). For after the sowing season comes the harvest. And if you've sown a lot of wild oats, you're in for some pretty bare cupboards.

If you're at all thinking about sowing some wild oats of your own, Hebrews 13:4 is the farmer's almanac you need to consult before you do. This verse contains two imperatives and a warning that reads like the skull-and-crossbones label on a jar of poison: HARMFUL OR FATAL IF SWALLOWED.

> Let marriage be held in honor among all, and let the marriage bed be undefiled; for fornicators and adulterers God will judge.

"Let Marriage Be Held in Honor"

At the writing of this letter to the Hebrews, there were many who held a low view of marriage. The ascetics despised marriage, advocating celibacy or castration in preference to a connubial relationship. Today marriage is dishonored in a different but equally demeaning way. Today marriage is looked on by some as an antiquated institution that inhibits the full development of self. The marriage vows are viewed as just words and the marriage certificate as just a piece of paper.

But simply because an institution is old, it doesn't follow that it is outdated. God looked down on man in the Garden and said that it was not good for him to be alone without a mate. His assessment still stands. And so does His institution.

It's our responsibility to protect and preserve that institution. How do we do that? The next command tells us.

"Let the Marriage Bed Be Undefiled"

Marriage is neither defiling, nor is it to be defiled. The Greek word for *undefiled* means "free from contamination." We defile our marital relationship when we become sexually intimate with anyone but our mate.

We may not be able to reverse the destructive trends that threaten other people's marriages, but we can do something to preserve the purity of our own. We can be faithful to our mates. That's how we show honor to the relationship. We give it sanctity and exclusivity when we're sexually faithful.

Paul provides the rationale for sexual purity in 1 Corinthians 6:16–20.

> Or do you not know that the one who joins himself to a harlot is one body with her? For He says, "The two will become one flesh." But the one who joins himself to the Lord is one spirit with Him. Flee immorality. Every other sin that a man commits is outside the body, but the immoral man sins against his own body. Or do you not know that your body is a temple of the Holy Spirit who is in you, whom you have from God, and that you are not your own? For you have been bought with a price: therefore glorify God in your body.[2]

Sexual immorality can never be contained to simply physical consequences because it is not merely a physical act. It involves the whole person—body, emotions, will, and spirit. And it affects the whole person. The memory becomes permanently etched with the experience, the conscience becomes scarred, and the spirit becomes polluted.

2. See also Galatians 5:16–19 and 1 Thessalonians 4:4–7.

"Fornicators and Adulterers God Will Judge"

The writer names two things that destroy the sanctity of sexuality within marriage: adultery and fornication. *Adultery* is a specific term that refers to extramarital relations. *Fornication* is a more general term that includes all forms of sexual impurity and immorality. Both incur God's judgment.

The first image that probably comes to mind when reading about God's judgment is one of fire and brimstone. Although God did punish Sodom and Gomorrah like that, His more characteristic way of meting out judgment is through our conscience. Notice how God put pressure on David's conscience after he committed adultery with Bathsheba.

> When I kept silent about my sin, my body wasted away
> Through my groaning all day long.
> For day and night Thy hand was heavy upon me;
> My vitality was drained away as with the fever heat of
> summer.
> (Ps. 32:3–4)

The drying up of life is the judgment of God. He saps our vitality. He withers our leaves. He makes brittle our branches. Hardly the picture of a fruitful life.

Heeding God's Counsel: Scriptural Answer

What does it take to obey these commands and escape God's judgment? What does it take to cultivate a marriage that blossoms with beauty and fragrance? What does it take to have a fruitful life?

In a word, *commitment.* Commitment to honoring marriage. Commitment to purity.

That means no compromise with your culture when the shifting standards of society are at odds with the firm standards of God. Remember, God is the one who sits on the throne—not the best-selling author or the most popular talk show host or the biggest box office star.

Majority opinion may rule in America, but God rules heaven and earth. He has the power to veto any opinion—no matter how popular, no matter how prevailing. And the rap of His gavel is the final one.

Living Insights STUDY ONE

Proverbs is largely the instruction of a father to his son regarding the practical skill of living life. One of the things the father warns his son about is the enticing lure of the adulterous woman (7:6–27). Later in the book there is a description of an excellent wife (31:10–31). In the following charts, contrast the qualities of the two women.

Qualities of the Adulterous Woman

Qualities of an Excellent Wife

Like a diamond against a black velvet backdrop, the facets of the excellent wife's character sparkle in contrast to the dark, manipulative character of the adulterous woman.

Now read Proverbs 5:15–20 and turn it into a prayer list for your own marriage. To give you a little help in being "exhilarated always" with your mate's love, read the Song of Solomon, picking out principles for improving your relationship.

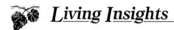

Living Insights

What does it take to fulfill the command given us in Hebrews 13:4? In a word, it takes *commitment.* Probably no passage of Scripture outlines the marriage commitment as clearly as Ephesians 5:22–33.

- From that passage describe how the wife should express her commitment to her husband.

____

____

- If you are a wife, what can you do specifically to demonstrate your commitment to your husband, based on the above answer?

____

____

- Now, what does the passage say about how a husband should express his commitment to his wife?

____

____

- If you are a husband, what can you do specifically to demonstrate your commitment to your wife, based on the above answer?

____

____

- How did Christ demonstrate His commitment to the church?

____

____

Look again at Ephesians 5:22–33. Use it as an opportunity to renew your vows by praying for your mate and for your commitment to your marriage.

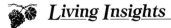

Chapter 15

COMMITMENT AND CONTENTMENT

(PART TWO)

Hebrews 13:5–6

The first part of this study concerned *marital commitment.* The second part, which we will examine today, concerns *material contentment.*

Just as commitment is the key to a marriage relationship, so contentment is the key to our relationship with finances.

The New Testament talks a lot about our relationship with money and material things. And over and over, the same theme keeps popping up—contentment.

> Not that I speak from want; for I have learned to be content in whatever circumstances I am. I know how to get along with humble means, and I also know how to live in prosperity; in any and every circumstance I have learned the secret of being filled and going hungry, both of having abundance and suffering need. (Phil. 4:11–12)

> But godliness actually is a means of great gain, when accompanied by contentment. For we have brought nothing into the world, so we cannot take anything out of it either. And if we have food and covering, with these we shall be content. (1 Tim. 6:6–8)

But this is opposite from the message the media sends us. It tells us to master our possibilities—not to be content with our circumstances.

Today we want to learn what it means to be content and why it is so important. For if there is a lack of contentment in our life, a vacuum is formed and anxiety comes rushing in to fill it (see Matt. 6:24–34). And when we are anxious, we become like Martha clanking around in the kitchen—distracted from the Lord by all our preparations.

Contentment in Hebrews

Hebrews 13:5–6 gives not only the admonition to be content but also the rationale behind it.

> Let your character be free from the love of money, being content with what you have; for He Himself has said, "I will never desert you, nor will I ever forsake you," so that we confidently say,
>
> "The Lord is my helper, I will not be
> afraid.
> What shall man do to me?"

"Let Your Character Be Free from the Love of Money"

The rich have an advantage over the poor in that they *know* money can't buy happiness. It can make life more comfortable and more convenient, but it can't make it happier. Often the have-nots wrestle with a lust for money more than the haves. And they don't find any relief in the media-driven hype that says the good life is the lifestyle of the rich and famous. Because that's more a Tinsel Town illusion than it is truth.

The Bible is clear: it's not money or the lack of it that's the problem—it's the *love* of it.

> For the love of money is a root of all sorts of evil, and some by longing for it have wandered away from the faith, and pierced themselves with many a pang. (1 Tim. 6:10)

The caveat expressed in 1 Timothy 6 is not addressed to the rich but to "those who want to get rich" (v. 9). It warns of the fall that so often accompanies the unbridled pursuit of riches by those who wish for the prestige money affords, who yearn for the security it promises, who lust for the power it brings, who long for the ease and comfort it provides.

Remember the statement in Galatians 5:1? "It was for freedom that Christ set us free." But when we love money, we become its slave. And when we enter its servitude, we find it becomes a harsh and exacting taskmaster. Not only that, it tolerates no rivals. It is so jealous that it will cause us to turn our back on our relationship with God (Matt. 6:24).

The solution, however, is not a vow of poverty. The solution is to make Jesus the Lord of our lives. To love only Him. To cling only to Him. To worship and serve only Him.

"Being Content with What You Have"

Contentment keeps us from being crabby about our cupboards, regardless of how bare they are. It helps us to be thankful for what we've got, rather than critical about what we don't have. As one commentator wrote:

> The avaricious man is never content: ungenerous and grasping, he always wants more and is always afraid of losing what he has. How different from the serenity of the true Christian who knows that, having Christ, he lacks nothing that is essential for his well-being (cf. Ps. 23:1). Paul, destitute of worldly possessions, sublimely speaks of himself "as having nothing, and yet possessing everything" (2 Cor. 6:10). "I have learned," he assures his friends in Philippi, "in whatever state I am, to be content" (Phil. 4:11). His is the true imitation of the Master, who on earth had no place of his own where he might rest his head (Mt. 8:20), who taught that "a man's life does not consist in the abundance of his possessions" (Lk. 12:15), and who advised his disciples to lay up treasure for themselves in heaven rather than on earth (Mt. 6:19f.).[1]

Contentment stems from a realization that all we have is ultimately a gracious provision from the hand of God—not merely from the sweat of our own brow or the skill of our brain.

Contentment also arises from our ability to see the difference between the cost of something and its true value. Henry David Thoreau put this in perspective when he said: "The cost of a thing is the amount of what I will call life which is required to be exchanged for it, immediately or in the long run."[2] Christ showed how this cost-to-value formula should affect the eternal decisions we make on earth in the parables of the hidden treasure and the pearl of great value (Matt. 13:44–46, see also 16:24–27).

"I Will Never Desert You, Nor Will I Ever Forsake You"

The reason we should be content with what we have is introduced by the causal connective "for" in the middle of Hebrews 13:5. We should be content, not because of the money we have, but

1. Philip Edgcumbe Hughes, A *Commentary on the Epistle to the Hebrews* (Grand Rapids, Mich.: William B. Eerdmans Publishing Co., 1977), pp. 567–68.

2. Henry David Thoreau, *Thoreau: Walden and Other Writings*, ed. Joseph Wood Krutch (New York, N.Y.: Bantam Books, 1962), p. 128.

because we have the continual presence of God. In verses 5 and 6 the writer to the Hebrews quotes from two Old Testament passages, Joshua 1:5 and Psalm 118:6.

In Joshua 1:5, we turn back the annals of time to a heroic chapter of Israel's history. As the nation stood on the banks of the Jordan overlooking the Promised Land, God commissioned the newly appointed leader, Joshua, to cross the river and conquer the land—a land peopled with giants and ruthless warriors. Joshua's strength was not in numbers or in armaments or strategy; it was in God going with them to prepare the way and to protect them.

That same assurance is echoed in Psalm 118:6 by the psalmist, who found himself surrounded by enemy nations. He went on to say:

> It is better to take refuge in the Lord
> Than to trust in man.
> It is better to take refuge in the Lord
> Than to trust in princes.
> (vv. 8–9)

That same strong presence, the writer to the Hebrews tells us, is ours today. And with that assurance we could write another verse of that psalm.

> It is better to take refuge in the Lord
> Than to trust in riches, real estate, and IRAs.
> It is better to take refuge in the Lord
> Than in the dollar, diamonds, and the Dow.

The point is, money and material possessions are unworthy of our love and our trust. At some point the bottom will drop out of the market, real estate will take a downturn, and the company you invested in to fund your retirement could go belly-up. The cycles are capricious. They can't be trusted.

In a world of fluctuating markets only one thing is a safe investment —the Lord. He's not subject to inflation or insolvency. He is the same yesterday, today, and forever.

> The name of the Lord is a strong tower;
> The righteous runs into it and is safe.
> A rich man's wealth is his strong city,
> And like a high wall in his own imagination.
> Before destruction the heart of man is haughty,
> But humility goes before honor.
> (Prov. 18:10–12)

Security can never be found in a safe-deposit box. It can be found only in the Lord. And that's the point the writer to the Hebrews is making.

Contentment in Your Life

Let's take this out of the theoretical and put it into the practical. How content are you with your salary? Are you critical of your company for not paying you more, for giving you only a token raise, for slipping only a measly Christmas bonus into your pay envelope?

How about where you live? Are you content with the home you live in? Do you feel you could live there the rest of your life and still be happy?

How about your possessions? Do you salivate every time a slick, new mail-order catalog comes to your home? Do you spend yourself into debt to gratify your desires, or are you content to wait on God's timing to provide for your needs?

Remember, contentment comes not in the accumulation of things but from the assurance that God will never leave or forsake you. And lest we forget this, it's stamped on every U.S. coin and printed on every piece of U.S. currency: In God We Trust.

Living Insights STUDY ONE

Here's a simple rule worth remembering: If it has a price tag, it won't bring lasting satisfaction. The answer to financial restlessness is contentment.

- Solomon discovered this lesson hundreds of years before the letter to the Hebrews was written. Let's examine some verses from his Old Testament book Ecclesiastes. As you read the passages, jot down your observations regarding the shallowness of materialism. Use this time for personal reflection.

Ecclesiastes 2:4–11, 5:10–17	
Observations on Materialism	Verse

Observations on Materialism	Verse

Living Insights STUDY TWO

When Henry David Thoreau withdrew from the world for two years to live on Walden Pond, he did so to simplify life and reduce it to its lowest common denominator. Ponder his words.

> I went to the woods because I wished to live deliberately, to front only the essential facts of life, and see if I could not learn what it had to teach, and not, when I came to die, discover that I had not lived. I did not wish to live what was not life, living is so dear, nor did I wish to practise resignation, unless it was quite necessary. I wanted to live deep and suck out all the marrow of life, to live so sturdily and Spartan-like as to put to rout all that was not life, to cut a broad swath and shave close, to drive life into a corner, and reduce it to its lowest terms.[3]

When a Christian reduces life to its lowest terms, it's Christ. He is the kernel. Everything else is husk. He, and He alone, is our basis for contentment.

> Whom have I in heaven but Thee?
> And besides Thee, I desire nothing on earth.
> (Ps. 73:25)

3. Thoreau, *Walden and Other Writings*, p. 172.

Chapter 16

My Responsibility to God-Appointed Leaders

Hebrews 13:7, 17; Matthew 15:1–14

In every area of life, leadership is essential—to chart the way, light the way, and lead the way. But sometimes we find our confidence in leadership shaken. We wonder if we haven't gone blindly down the wrong road, following some persuasive Pied Piper to our destruction.

When there is a crisis in leadership, there is a crumbling of credibility. When there is a breakdown of personal ethics in the lives of our leaders, there is a breach of public trust. And when we have been burned by a leader, it's difficult to warm up to the fiery rhetoric of the next person who steps up to the podium.

Nevertheless, leadership is as essential to religion as a captain is to the safe voyage of a ship. With it, we always run the risk of running aground on a reef. But without it, we would never even get out of port.

Analysis of Wrong Leadership

From the fall of the Roman Empire to the fall of a televangelist's empire, the thing that makes poor leaders topple is often power that has gone to their heads. Maybe they thought they were above the law. Maybe they thought no one would find out. Maybe they thought a noble end justified any notorious means used to achieve it. Whatever the case, the wreckage caused by their ungodly leadership is strewn throughout the pages of history.

As Christians we need to learn what God would have us do about bad leaders. Is there a way to evaluate them and prevent ourselves from becoming part of history's wreckage? Let's take a look at what Jesus had to say about the wrong type of leadership.

How Do We Spot Leadership That Is in Error?

Matthew 15 frames an incident that took place between Jesus and the religious leaders of His time, the Pharisees. And it's not a very flattering portrait.

> Then some Pharisees and scribes came to Jesus from Jerusalem, saying, "Why do Your disciples transgress

> the tradition of the elders? For they do not wash their hands when they eat bread." (vv. 1–2)

Alfred Edersheim gives us a glimpse of the tedious nature of the hand-washing tradition they were referring to.

> As the purifications were so frequent, and care had to be taken that the water had not been used for other purposes, or something fallen into it that might discolour or defile it, large vessels or jars were generally kept for the purpose . . . which must hold (at least) a quarter of a log—a measure equal to one and a half 'egg-shells.' . . . The water was poured on both hands, which must be free of anything covering them, such as gravel, mortar, [etc.]. The hands were lifted up, so as to make the water run to the wrist, in order to ensure that the whole hand was washed, and that the water polluted by the hand did not again run down the fingers. Similarly, each hand was rubbed with the other (the fist), provided the hand that rubbed had been affused. . . . In the 'first affusion,' . . . the water had to run down to the wrist. . . . If the water remained short of the wrist . . . the hands were not clean. . . . If the hands were 'defiled,' two affusions were required: the first, or 'first waters' . . . to remove the defilement, and the 'second,' or 'after waters' . . . to wash away the waters that had contracted the defilement of the hands.[1]

The ritual pedantry is hard enough to read, let alone to follow. But the religious leaders were punctilious about every jot and tittle of the observance. The problem was that they put the tradition of men on equal footing with the commandments of God. In fact, the Jews added more than six hundred laws to the original ten commandments.

The remainder of Matthew's account outlines three patterns found in ungodly leadership.

First: *Human opinion is honored above the Word of God.*

> And [Jesus] answered and said to them, "And why do you yourselves transgress the commandment of God for the sake of your tradition? For God said, 'Honor your father and mother,' and 'He who speaks evil of

1. Alfred Edersheim, *The Life and Times of Jesus the Messiah* (Grand Rapids, Mich.: William B. Eerdmans Publishing Co., 1959), vol. 2, pp. 11–12.

> father or mother, let him be put to death.' But you say, 'Whoever shall say to his father or mother, "Anything of mine you might have been helped by has been given to God," he is not to honor his father or his mother.' And thus you invalidated the word of God for the sake of your tradition." (vv. 3–6)

When those in leadership value human traditions, rituals, or rules as equal to or greater than the Word of God, then that leadership has gone awry.

Second: *Hypocrisy prevails over authenticity.* Jesus continues His rebuke:

> "You hypocrites, rightly did Isaiah prophesy of you, saying,
>
> 'This people honors Me with their lips,
> But their heart is far away from Me.
> But in vain do they worship Me,
> Teaching as doctrines the precepts of
> men.' "
>
> And after He called the multitude to Him, He said to them, "Hear, and understand. Not what enters into the mouth defiles the man, but what proceeds out of the mouth, this defiles the man." (vv. 7–11)

Authentic Christianity is a religion of the heart. When the heart is bad—regardless of how good the theology is—the religion is bad. The heart is what God judges—not our doctrinal statements or our rote confessions of faith.

Third: *Self-imposed rigidity is expressed rather than God-anointed sensitivity.*

> Then the disciples came and said to Him, "Do You know that the Pharisees were offended when they heard this statement?" But He answered and said, "Every plant which My heavenly Father did not plant shall be rooted up. Let them alone; they are blind guides of the blind. And if a blind man guides a blind man, both will fall into a pit." (vv. 12–14)

Jesus is saying that the Pharisees had become rigid in their worship and had lost the sensitivity of heart that keeps a person's spiritual life supple and responsive. The condition of their hearts affected the vision of their eyes. When their hearts became hard, their eyes became blind.

And when a leader goes blind spiritually, those who follow are destined for destruction. That is what happened in Jonestown not too many years ago—and it resulted in the cyanide suicides of more than nine hundred followers of the Reverend Jim Jones.

How Do We Handle Leadership That Is in Error?

Are we to keep following spiritual leaders who have, for whatever reason, wandered offtrack? Are we to support them and submit to them, looking the other way from their jaunts into infidelity and their narcissistic treks into themselves? Or are we to try to change them? For an answer, look at what Jesus taught in verse 14—"Let them alone."

If leaders exhibit these patterns, you are to drop them like a bad habit.

Response to God-Appointed Leadership

En route to Hebrews 13 let's pull into port at 1 Corinthians 1 to note something important about human leaders.

> I have been informed concerning you, my brethren, by Chloe's people, that there are quarrels among you. Now I mean this, that each one of you is saying, "I am of Paul," and "I of Apollos," and "I of Cephas," and "I of Christ." (vv. 11–12)

Notice the last group in the list, those who say "I am of Christ." Some people get so disillusioned with earthly leadership that they give up on it. They piously feel that they don't need anyone except Christ to lead them.

Only one problem—Christ Himself ordained leadership within His body to help it grow and mature.

> And He gave some as apostles, and some as prophets, and some as evangelists, and some as pastors and teachers, for the equipping of the saints for the work of service, to the building up of the body of Christ; until we all attain to the unity of the faith, and of the knowledge of the Son of God, to a mature man, to the measure of the stature which belongs to the fulness of Christ. (Eph. 4:11–13)

Regarding Past Models

As we come into the harbor of Hebrews 13, we want to wrap our moorings around verses 7 and 17. They will give us some solid advice regarding leadership. Let's first take a look at verse 7.

> Remember those who led you, who spoke the word of God to you; and considering the result of their conduct, imitate their faith.

There are two commands to be found in this verse—*remember* and *imitate.* Remember and imitate who? "Those who led you."

Close your eyes and take a mental trip back through the art gallery of your spiritual memory. Whose pictures are on those walls? Among them, surely, are a few that stand out. A Sunday school teacher, perhaps, who endured your antics and somehow got across to you the patience of God. Maybe a grandparent who filled your imagination with the stories of David and Goliath and Noah's ark. It may have been a youth worker who invested time and love in you, or just a friend who wouldn't let spiritual issues slide.

But what are we to do with our memories of these people? The verse says to "[consider] the result of their conduct." The word *consider* means "to look up a subject, to investigate, and to observe accurately." Don't just glance at those portraits and gloss over them in fond reminiscence. Stop and gaze at them. Recall what it was about that coach that made such a difference in your life; figure out how that pastor kept you coming back Sunday after Sunday. And imitate those things. Incorporate them into your life. Those kinds of role models are gifts from God . . . gifts that go on giving long after the person is gone from our lives.

Today's Exemplary Leaders

Let's go on to take a look at verse 17.

> Obey your leaders, and submit to them; for they keep watch over your souls, as those who will give an account. Let them do this with joy and not with grief, for this would be unprofitable for you.

Today's godly leaders may become tomorrow's heroes, even some who are now misunderstood, maligned, and rejected. Often, their true contribution isn't fully understood or appreciated until years after their death. What is God's counsel regarding such leaders today? To obey and submit to them.

Why? Because they keep watch over our souls. The verb *keep watch* literally means "to search for sleep." It's the picture of someone staying awake at night, of a person who is seeking sleep but can't find it, of a person so burdened with concern for others that it keeps this person awake at night.

Another detail that adds color to the verse is that the "they" is emphatic. The idea is "they *themselves* watch over you." It's not something they can leave at the office or delegate to their subordinates. When you stub your spiritual toe, they feel the pain shooting up their own leg.

Another reason we should submit to godly spiritual leaders is that they have to give an account of their stewardship over the flock of God, where they serve as shepherds, not hirelings (see John 10:11–15). They can't shrug off a wayward sheep and say, "So what? Who cares?" They are accountable to the owner of the sheepfold —not only for the ninety-nine which are safe but for the one that has wandered off.

The final reason we are to submit to our spiritual leaders is so they might be relieved of *grief*. The term means "to groan." There's probably no profession more emotionally enervating than pastoral work. It's filled with all kinds of groanings within the spirit that are often too deep for words.

If we resist this type of God-appointed leadership over our lives, we lose—it is "unprofitable" for us. And so, submitting becomes a matter not only of expedience—it is in our own best interest.

Some Overriding, Lasting Principles

As we look back over our shoulders to the road we've traveled today, three principles emerge. One, it's unbiblical to support wrong leadership, no matter how sincere it may appear. Two, it is unwise to recognize no leadership, no matter how comfortable it seems to feel. Three, it is unprofitable to resist right leadership, no matter how painful it may be.

Living Insights STUDY ONE

Submission to human leadership is an often misunderstood concept, whether that leadership is ecclesiastical or governmental. Let's expand our study to include the secular arena as well as the spiritual one.

- As you read the following passages, jot down some principles regarding your responsibility to your leaders.

My Responsibility to God-Appointed Leaders

Romans 13:1–7:

Hebrews 13:7, 17:

1 Peter 2:13–17:

Living Insights STUDY TWO

Here are some questions pertaining to leadership. Think through them carefully, writing down your conclusions in the space provided.

- Is it always right to support spiritual leadership? If not, what are the exceptions?

- Give some examples from the Bible of spiritual leadership that should have been followed but wasn't.

____

____

____

- Now give some examples of spiritual leadership that shouldn't have been followed but was.

____

____

____

- How does all this apply to a citizen of the United States? How about a citizen of Nazi Germany?

____

____

____

- How do you think this applied to a citizen of the Roman Empire in the first century?

____

____

____

Chapter 17

CHANGELESS TRUTHS IN A SHIFTLESS WORLD

Hebrews 13:8–16

The ancient Greek philosopher Heraclitus built his system of thought on the principle that "nothing endures but change."[1] He contended that everything is in a state of flux, and he illustrated his point by stating that "it is not possible to step twice into the same river."[2]

From something as subtle as the changing currents in a river to something as dramatic as the changing of the seasons, all of life does appear to be in flux.

Adding to this endless cycle of change are our fads and fashions. Remember when . . . there was the dry look, the wet look, and then the buzz . . . there were white socks, dark socks, and then no socks . . . there was the twist, the jerk, and then disco?

We have only to drag out our high school yearbooks to chronicle the changes in our own lives. From the length of our sideburns to the width of our ties, we're constantly changing.

Sometimes the changes come slowly; other times, abruptly. Pollsters have documented that we change our jobs every five years, our friends every four years, our cars every three years, our churches every two years, our styles every year, and our minds every month!

Washington Irving wrote:

> There is a certain relief in change, even though it be from bad to worse; as I have found in travelling in a stage-coach, that it is often a comfort to shift one's position and be bruised in a new place.[3]

This constant shifting—which is characteristic of the entire human race—demonstrates that we are *mutable,* which Webster

1. *Bartlett's Familiar Quotations,* 14th ed., rev. and enl., ed. Emily Morison Beck (Boston, Mass.: Little, Brown and Co., 1968), p. 77.

2. *Bartlett's Familiar Quotations,* p. 77.

3. As quoted in *The Home Book of Quotations,* 10th ed., selected and arranged by Burton Stevenson (New York, N.Y.: Dodd, Mead and Co., 1967), p. 231.

defines as "prone to change: inconstant . . . capable of change."[4] With the currents of change washing over and around us so swiftly, it's comforting to know that there's a boulder in the midst of that river that is immutable. The prophet Malachi put it succinctly: "For I, the Lord, do not change" (Mal. 3:6a).

The Doctrine of Immutability

A. W. Tozer clarifies this concept of God's immutability in his book *The Knowledge of the Holy.*

> To say that God is immutable is to say that He never differs from Himself. The concept of a growing or developing God is not found in the Scriptures. . . .
>
> God cannot change for the better. Since He is perfectly holy, He has never been less holy than He is now and can never be holier than He is and has always been. Neither can God change for the worse. Any deterioration within the unspeakably holy nature of God is impossible. Indeed I believe it impossible even to think of such a thing, for the moment we attempt to do so, the object about which we are thinking is no longer God but something else and someone less than He. . . .
>
> The immutability of God appears in its most perfect beauty when viewed against the mutability of men. In God no change is possible; in men change is impossible to escape. Neither the man is fixed nor his world, but he and it are in constant flux.[5]

Scriptural support for this doctrine of the unchanging nature of God can be found in such passages as Hebrews 13:8 and James 1:17.

> Jesus Christ is the same yesterday and today, yes and forever.

> Every good thing bestowed and every perfect gift is from above, coming down from the Father of lights, with whom there is no variation, or shifting shadow.

In contrast to His creatures, God is not given to moods. Our Lord remains constant in His love for us. He isn't fickle. He doesn't say one thing and mean another. He doesn't change His standards

4. *Webster's New Collegiate Dictionary,* see "mutable."

5. A. W. Tozer, *The Knowledge of the Holy* (San Francisco, Calif.: Harper and Row, Publishers, 1961), pp. 49–50.

in midstream. He doesn't sign a contract one day and break it the next. With Him there is no variation or shifting shadow. He is the same yesterday, today, and forever.

Warning against Heresy

The immutability of God, as articulated in Hebrews 13:8, is what keeps us from being swept away by the swift, turbid currents of fluctuating doctrines mentioned in verse 9.

> Do not be carried away by varied and strange teachings; for it is good for the heart to be strengthened by grace, not by foods, through which those who were thus occupied were not benefited.

The word *varied* is from the Greek *poikilos,* from which we get the word *polka dot.* This word pictures a variety of colors that please the eye and titillate the senses. They may be bright red dots that stimulate our passions, cool blue ones that appeal to our intellects, brilliant gold ones that promise fortune, or gray ones that try to make us compromise the black-and-white issues of Scripture.

These "varied and strange teachings" basically attack the principle of grace—which is God's gift of spiritual strength. It is made available to us through what His Son accomplished for us on the cross, not from "foods" or some ceremonial substance or from tangible trinkets, as the last part of verse 9 shows.

And emphasizing these externals is like feeding people husks of hollow religion instead of nourishing kernels of truth. The result? There's no benefit, no health, no strength. Why? Because there is no true substance . . . there is no grace.

Have you ever looked deeply into the faces of folks who've been fed a steady diet of husks? Their eyes seem a little sunken; their cheeks, a little hollow; their skin, a little pale.

Hardly a health-club ad for the abundant Christian life, is it? What is lacking in the diet is the Bread of Life, slathered with His grace.

Look carefully at verses 10–16.

> We have an altar, from which those who serve the tabernacle have no right to eat. For the bodies of those animals whose blood is brought into the holy place by the high priest as an offering for sin, are burned outside the camp. Therefore Jesus also, that He might sanctify the people through His own blood, suffered outside

> the gate. Hence, let us go out to Him outside the camp, bearing His reproach. For here we do not have a lasting city, but we are seeking the city which is to come. Through Him then, let us continually offer up a sacrifice of praise to God, that is, the fruit of lips that give thanks to His name. And do not neglect doing good and sharing; for with such sacrifices God is pleased.

Underscore the pronouns, and you'll see two groups of people contrasted: verse 10—"*we . . . those*"; verse 13—"*us*"; verses 14–15 —"*we . . . we . . . us.*"

The contrast is between those who find Christ fully sufficient and those who opt for empty religion. In these verses we can glean a list of four specifics that are involved in the lives of those who embrace grace through Jesus Christ.

Four Things Only Christians Possess

Those who abandon their lives to fervently follow Jesus Christ have four things: an altar to use (v. 10), a reproach to bear (vv. 11–13), a city to seek (v. 14), and a sacrifice to offer (vv. 15–16). Let's take a look at each one.

An Altar to Use

> We have an altar, from which those who serve the tabernacle have no right to eat. (v. 10)

This verse refers to the cross, where Christ's sacrificial offering was made. Those who seek fulfillment by serving the tabernacle—that is, by worshiping in form only—"have no right to eat" at that altar. To *them,* the crucified Christ means nothing. But to *us,* He is our altar.

A Reproach to Bear

> For the bodies of those animals whose blood is brought into the holy place by the high priest as an offering for sin, are burned outside the camp. Therefore Jesus also, that He might sanctify the people through His own blood, suffered outside the gate. Hence, let us go out to Him outside the camp, bearing His reproach. (vv. 11–13)

This passage makes a connection between the animal sacrifices of the tabernacle and the sacrifice of Christ. The point of comparison is that both sacrifices were made outside the community—the first outside the camp of Israel and the second outside the gates of Jerusalem.[6] In this comparison the writer sees an instructive picture, as William Barclay explains.

> Christ was crucified outside the gate. He was exiled from men and numbered with the transgressors. Therein the writer to the Hebrews sees a picture. We, too, have to sever ourselves from the life of the world and be willing to bear the same reproach as Christ bore. The isolation and the humiliation may come to the Christian as they came to his Saviour.[7]

How easy it would have been for those first-century Jewish Christians to settle comfortably within the community, rubbing elbows at the dinner table with the Judaizers and maintaining the status quo. But there is a price to pay for identifying with Christ; there's a stigma to live with, a reproach to bear.

Hebrews 11:24–26 gives a beautiful example of a man who knew this and lived it.

> By faith Moses, when he had grown up, refused to be called the son of Pharaoh's daughter; choosing rather to endure ill-treatment with the people of God, than to enjoy the passing pleasures of sin; considering the reproach of Christ greater riches than the treasures of Egypt; for he was looking to the reward.

The closer we align ourselves with Christ, the closer we align ourselves with the sufferings of His cross. Taking up that cross, we bear His reproach through enduring abuse, misunderstanding, and persecution (Phil. 1:29, 2 Tim. 3:12, 1 Pet. 4:12–19).

6. "The carcasses of the beasts slaughtered at the altar on the Day of Atonement were carried forth outside the camp, in accordance with the prescription of Leviticus 16:27, and completely burned. The camp ground was holy ground, but the ground outside the camp was unholy ground; consequently, ceremonial cleansing was required before a man could return to the camp from outside (as we see from Lev. 16:26 and 28). . . . By suffering outside the gate, moreover, Jesus identifies himself with the world in its unholiness. While we are unable to draw near to God because of our sin, God draws near to us in the person of his Holy One who on our unholy ground makes his holiness available to us in exchange for our sin which he bears and for which he atones on the cross." Philip Edgcumbe Hughes, *A Commentary on the Epistle to the Hebrews* (Grand Rapids, Mich.: William B. Eerdmans Publishing Co., 1977), pp. 578–79.

7. William Barclay, *The Letter to the Hebrews*, rev. ed., The Daily Study Bible Series (Philadelphia, Pa.: Westminster Press, 1976), p. 198.

A City to Seek

> For here we do not have a lasting city, but we are seeking the city which is to come. (Heb. 13:14)

If we're busy constructing some Tower of Babel to create a name for ourselves, it won't last. Empires are fleeting, whether they are personal, political, or financial ones (see Isa. 40:6–8, 15–17). The only city to seek is the city that lasts, the one sought by the storied heroes of the faith so many millennia ago (see Heb. 11:13–16).

A Sacrifice to Offer

> Through Him then, let us continually offer up a sacrifice of praise to God, that is, the fruit of lips that give thanks to His name. And do not neglect doing good and sharing; for with such sacrifices God is pleased. (13:15–16)

Since we have no earthly altar, no earthly identity, and no earthly place of citizenship, does that mean we have no sacrifice to offer? No. As verse 15 says, we can offer "a sacrifice of praise." Verse 16 expands the list to include "doing good" and "sharing." God doesn't want lip service. He wants us to put shoes on our words. He wants us to walk our talk. And if our walk is to make any difference in the lives of those around us, we must go the extra mile. We must make the sacrifice, whether it's our time, our energy, or our money.

Means to Practicality

To put shoe leather on what we've learned, tack down these three principles to the soles of your thinking.

First: *A changing world emphasizes our need for a changeless Christ.* To keep from being swept away by treacherous currents, we need a solid rock to cling to; we need a Savior who isn't capricious, a Savior we can count on.

Second: *A changeless Christ redirects our desire toward a grace relationship.* When we find in Christ all that God needed, then we find in Christ all that we need. And when we realize that all we need flows freely from Christ, then we start to operate by grace. Then we start looking at ourselves as recipients of unmerited favor rather than wage earners of works.

Third: *A grace relationship strengthens our hope in a secure eternity.* If getting to the city of God were based on works, none of us would know for certain whether we'd get there. But if the basis is grace, it's like having the key to eternity placed in a safe-deposit box in heaven. Then we don't have to worry about losing our salvation, because it's not in our hands to begin with.

In an era where families are as likely to be scattered across the country as they are to stay in their hometown, where the jobs we trained for in college are already obsolete, where the childhood our kids are experiencing looks nothing like the one we enjoyed . . . isn't it good to know there's one thing that will never change? Isn't it comforting to plant our feet firmly on God's steadfast nature and let the currents of the world swirl past us? Lean hard on His rock-steady character; cling to His never-changing love. It's one thing you can count on.

Living Insights STUDY ONE

In this study we've learned about the blessing of God's immutability. It's so encouraging to know that He is our anchor in this swiftly changing world.

- In some of our earlier lessons, we used the study method of paraphrasing. Let's use this skill once again, in Hebrews 13:8–16, but this time paraphrase the passage by turning it into our own personal prayer list. We'll do verse 8 to get you started, and then you can do the rest.

Paraphrase of Hebrews 13:8–16

Dear Lord,

Thank You that You are the same yesterday, today, and forever. Thank You that You don't change, that You remain the same, that You're someone I can count on. Thank You for being a rock in this fast moving world of ours. . . .

Living Insights — STUDY TWO

"Through Him then, let us continually offer up a sacrifice of praise to God" (Heb. 13:15a). Have you taken time lately to praise God? Let's do it now.

- One of the best vehicles of praise is a hymnbook. Select a few of your favorites and pray them back to God in praise. Here are a few suggestions for starters:

"A Mighty Fortress Is Our God"

"Great Is Thy Faithfulness"

"The Solid Rock"

"Holy, Holy, Holy"

"Immortal, Invisible, God Only Wise"

"How Great Thou Art"

Chapter 18

Daring the Risk of Reach

Hebrews 13:18–19, Ephesians 6:11–20, Mark 9:17–29

One Sunday morning Peter Marshall, much-loved Scottish immigrant-pastor and chaplain of the United States Senate, paraphrased the poignant ending of Erich Maria Remarque's *All Quiet on the Western Front.*

> It was an afternoon in the early summer; there was a strange quiet on the battlefield.
> In the bright sunshine, the air was balmy and had a breath of garden in it.
>
> By some grotesque miracle, a bird was singing somewhere near at hand.
> On the firing step, with his rifle lying in a groove in the parapet, stood a private soldier in field-gray, his uniform stained with mud and blood.
>
> On his face, so young yet strangely marked with the lines of war that made him look old, was a wistful faraway expression.
>
> He was enjoying the sunshine and the quiet of this strange lull in the firing.
> The heavy guns had been silent—there was no sound to break the eerie stillness.
>
> Suddenly a butterfly fluttered into view and alighted on the ground almost at the end of his rifle.
> It was a strange visitor to a battleground—so out of place—so out of keeping with the grim setting
> rifles and bayonets
> barbed wire and parapets
> shell holes and twisted bodies.
>
> But there it was—a gorgeous creature, the wings like gold leaf splashed with carmine,
> swaying in the warm breath of spring.
>
> As the war-weary youngster watched the butterfly, he was no longer a private in field-gray.
> He was a boy once more, fresh and clean, swinging

through a field in sunny Saxony, knee-deep in clover
buttercups
and daisies.

That strange visitor to the front-line trench recalled to him the joys of his boyhood, when he had collected butterflies.
It spoke to him of days of peace.
It was a symbol of the lovelier things of life.
It was the emblem of the eternal, a reminder that there was still beauty and peace in the world—that somewhere there was color and fragility
and perfume
and flowers
and gardens.

He forgot the enemy a few hundred yards across no man's land.
He forgot the danger and privation and suffering.
He forgot everything as he watched that butterfly.

With all the hunger in his heart,
with the resurrection of dreams and visions that he thought were gone, he reached out his hand toward that butterfly.

His fingers moved slowly, cautiously, lest he frighten away this visitor to the battlefield.
In showing one kind of caution, he forgot another.
The butterfly was just beyond his reach—so he stretched, forgetting that watchful eyes were waiting for a target.

He brought himself out slowly—with infinite care and patience—until now he had just a little distance to go.
He could almost touch the wings that were so lovely.

And then . . . ping . . . *ing* . . . *ing* . . . *ing* . . .
A sniper's bullet found its mark.
The stretching fingers relaxed . . .
the hand dropped flat on the ground . . .
For the private soldier in field-gray, the war was over.

An official bulletin issued that afternoon said that
"All was quiet on the Western Front . . ."
And for a boy in field-gray it was a quiet that no guns would ever break.[1]

1. Peter Marshall, *John Doe, Disciple,* ed. Catherine Marshall (New York, N.Y.: McGraw-Hill Book Co., 1963), pp. 139–42. Used by permission. Chosen Books will be reissuing this excellent resource in 1990 under the new title *His Hand on Your Shoulder.*

Many of us are like that boy in the parapet, so battered and bloodied from the battles of life that our dreams have been driven into cynical silence—by all the stoves that have burned us, all the hateful people who have hurt us, all the huge barriers that have intimidated us. Yet no sniper's bullet has been quite able to put those dreams to death. Within each of us there still exists a quiet and childlike confidence in God we seem to have been born with.

Oh, it may be slumbering. It may have been long years since we've felt it stir. But it's still there, waiting to be awakened. Our only trouble is that we are better students of the battlefield than we are of butterflies. We hear the words of our enemy all the time, playing back the accusations of guilt, memories of wrong, failures of yesterday. And they come like flaming missiles, screaming, "Stop reaching! Stop asking! Stop praying! There are no butterflies!"

But butterflies do exist. And reaching for them, risking for them, is essential to life. Not to the physical, temporal, muddy life in the trenches, but to the life of the heart.

A Scene of Warfare

The World Wars are over now. For most of us, soldiering in the trenches seems an unlikely prospect. Yet a war rages in and around us all the time. We stand, walk, and sleep on a battlefield every day. We hear the zing of the bullets and often feel their debilitating sting, but since we don't see the enemy uniform, we don't call it a war. But invisible warfare is warfare, all the same. And it requires protective equipment—also invisible. Paul tells us about it in Ephesians 6.

> Put on the full armor of God, that you may be able to stand firm against the schemes of the devil. For our struggle is not against flesh and blood, but against the rulers, against the powers, against the world forces of this darkness, against the spiritual forces of wickedness in the heavenly places. Therefore, take up the full armor of God, that you may be able to resist in the evil day, and having done everything, to stand firm. Stand firm therefore, having girded your loins with truth, and having put on the breastplate of righteousness, and having shod your feet with the preparation of the gospel of peace; in addition to all, taking up the shield of faith with which you will be able to extinguish all the flaming missiles of the evil one. And take the helmet of salvation, and the sword of the Spirit, which is the word of God. (vv. 11–17)

With the equipment come orders for fighting this invisible war. You may be surprised to find that the combat isn't hand-to-hand—this is one war that is won on our knees.

> With all prayer and petition pray at all times in the Spirit, and with this in view, be on the alert with all perseverance and petition for all the saints, and pray on my behalf, that utterance may be given to me in the opening of my mouth, to make known with boldness the mystery of the gospel, for which I am an ambassador in chains; that in proclaiming it I may speak boldly, as I ought to speak. (vv. 18–20)

We need to pray not only for ourselves, but for our fellow soldiers, especially those on the front lines. Even the writer of these commands admits his need for the support of the whole battalion.

A Cry for Help

If we turn a few pages to the book of Hebrews, we hear another request for a rear guard of prayer.

> Pray for us, for we are sure that we have a good conscience, desiring to conduct ourselves honorably in all things. (13:18)

When someone asks for prayer, we tend to think there must be something wrong. Sometimes that's true, but not always. The word *desiring* in this verse gives us a clue to the reason for this writer's request. Rather weak in the translation, in its original form it carried the idea of being "bound and determined" to do something—in his case, to live a godly life.

The writer, though, isn't so spiritually minded that he doesn't understand human nature. Read on to the next verse.

> And I urge you all the more to do this, that I may be restored to you the sooner. (v. 19)

How many times have you promised to pray for someone and either forgotten all about it or just tucked it quickly in as you were falling asleep? The needs of the sick weigh heavily on our minds, but the needs of a healthy, active soldier . . . well, a mere desire for reinforcement doesn't get our attention. If you've ever done battle on the ground, however, you know how welcome is the sight of a plane with your insignia coming in for a landing with food and new artillery.

An Announcement to Ponder

For many of us, our battlefields take the form of impossible situations in which we desperately need reinforcements. What is your battlefield right now? Maybe it's your marriage; perhaps it's your job. Or it could be your finances or your health. Whatever it is, you probably feel like the bullets are flying and there's not a butterfly in sight. But take heart. Mark 9 breathes a breeze of fresh air across a war zone choked with the dust of combat. Its story takes place in the days of Jesus, when physicians were scarce and medicines rudimentary. A serious disease usually finished people off, and demons seemed impossible to fight. But here we see the faithful father of a demonically sick boy—a father who kept reaching for the butterfly.

> "Teacher, I brought You my son, possessed with a spirit which makes him mute; and whenever it seizes him, it dashes him to the ground and he foams at the mouth, and grinds his teeth, and stiffens out. And I told Your disciples to cast it out, and they could not do it." (vv. 17–18)

As if that doesn't paint a horrible enough picture, the details get even worse. But Jesus isn't daunted by this pathetic sight. His words to the man contain only fatigue and honest reproof.

> "O unbelieving generation, how long shall I be with you? How long shall I put up with you? Bring him to Me!" And they brought the boy to Him. And when he saw Him, immediately the spirit threw him into a convulsion, and falling to the ground, he began rolling about and foaming at the mouth. And [Jesus] asked his father, "How long has this been happening to him?" And he said, "From childhood. And it has often thrown him both into the fire and into the water to destroy him. But if You can do anything, take pity on us and help us!" And Jesus said to him, "'If You can!' All things are possible to him who believes." Immediately the boy's father cried out and began saying, "I do believe; help my unbelief." (vv. 19–24)

In the midst of a raging battle for his son's life, that father caught a glimpse of a butterfly. And when he stretched out a helpless hand to take hold of it, he found the strong hand of the Savior.

> And when Jesus saw that a crowd was rapidly gathering, He rebuked the unclean spirit, saying to it, "You deaf and dumb spirit, I command you, come out of

> him and do not enter him again." And after crying out and throwing him into terrible convulsions, it came out; and the boy became so much like a corpse that most of them said, "He is dead!" But Jesus took him by the hand and raised him; and he got up. (vv. 25–27)

Watching this scene was a group of frustrated men—the disciples.

> And when He had come into the house, His disciples began questioning Him privately, "Why could we not cast it out?" And He said to them, "This kind cannot come out by anything but prayer." (vv. 28–29)

Jesus gave them an exclusive solution for an impossible situation: prayer.

Butterflies in Battlefields

In all our lives, there are certain situations that require us to risk reaching for the butterflies—situations that can't be solved by anything short of reaching out to God in prayer. Christ's words to that faithful father are no less true for us today: "All things are possible to him who believes." That's not a blanket promise that we will receive exactly what we ask for. It means that if we turn our impossible situations over to Him, He will take the burden of the battle and renew our dream of the butterfly. He'll give us hope to survive.

There are two lasting principles we should remember from this idea of butterflies in battlefields.

First: *In life's battles, there are snipers of fear that human hearts cannot ignore.* Unlike that soldier on the parapet, we are usually all too conscious of the dangers around us. We fear being hurt, being rejected, failing, having our faults exposed. Yet just beyond those fears is a butterfly, and unless we take the risk of reaching past them in prayer, we'll never glimpse the face of God.

Second: *In life's battles, there are butterflies of faith that natural eyes cannot envision.* That's why prayer is crucial, to give you the eyes of faith. If you call on unbelievers around you, they'll just remind you of the stench of the trenches. If you try to crawl over the parapet, they're likely to pull you back by your belt loops. But prayer will lure you over that earthen barrier to the vision of greener fields beyond the battle.

Are you fighting a seemingly impossible battle right now, even as you read? Are you crouched behind the parapet, dodging bullets and taking aim? If so, keep a lookout for the butterfly. It's there, just beyond your reach. And if you're fearful and hesitant to stretch out your hand, take hope from Peter Marshall's closing words.

> There is always a risk—when you reach for the beautiful.
> When you reach out for the lovelier
>   finer
>   more fragrant things of life—
> there is always a risk—and you can't escape it.
>
> The risk is what makes the Christian life exciting.
>   It is thrilling—make no mistake about it.
>   It is an adventure.
> As long as we live in this world, there will always be
> a risk in reach.[2]

Living Insights STUDY ONE

As Christians, we are involved in a warfare that's more intense than one fought with gunpowder, rockets, and artillery. The war in which we are engaged is invisible, and special pieces of armor are necessary for our survival.

- Turn again to Ephesians 6:11–20. Let's analyze the Christian's armor. In the space provided, write down each piece of armor, the portion of the body it protects, and the significance of how each piece of armor relates to that part of the body. Stick with the text, but think creatively!

The Christian's Armor

Piece of armor: ____________ Part protected: ____________

Significance: ______________________________

____

____

Piece of armor: ____________ Part protected: ____________

Significance: ______________________________

____

____

2. Marshall, *John Doe, Disciple,* p. 142.

Piece of armor: ____________ Part protected: ____________

Significance: ______________________________________

____

____

Piece of armor: ____________ Part protected: ____________

Significance: ______________________________________

____

____

Piece of armor: ____________ Part protected: ____________

Significance: ______________________________________

____

____

Piece of armor: ____________ Part protected: ____________

Significance: ______________________________________

____

____

Living Insights STUDY TWO

As long as we live in this world, there will always be a risk in reaching. Whether it is reaching out to others on a horizontal level or reaching out on their behalf vertically through prayer, reach means risk.

- Are you ready to dare the risk of reach? Take some time to ponder that question and all its implications. If your answer is yes, then finish the following sentences.

  I will risk reach by ______________________________

  ____

  ____.

I will reach out to ____

____

____ .

I will reach out to God by _________________________________

____

____ .

Chapter 19

Equipped to Do His Will

Hebrews 13:20–21

In the *Second Lieutenant's Handbook,* printed for soldiers during World War II, there is a detailed list of equipment issued to make every soldier field-ready:

Bag, Musette-Bag Field Canvas
Belt, Web
Canteen, Cup and Cover
Meat Can, Knife, Fork, Spoon
Wash Basin, Folding Canvas
Case (Dispatch)
Helmet, Trench
Tags, Identification
Mask, Gas
Pistol, .45
Magazine, Filled
Ammunition (Ball Pistol Cal. .45)
Suspenders, Official Type
Pouch, First-Aid
Watch
Compass
Field Message Book
Packet, First-Aid[1]

It would be unthinkable to send a soldier into combat without the necessary supplies. For not only is his success on the line, but his very survival.

It would be equally unthinkable for God to enlist us into His service without equipping us to do His will.

In his benedictory farewell, the writer to the Hebrews broaches this issue.

1. John R. Craf, *Second Lieutenant's Handbook* (Stanford, Calif.: Stanford University Press, 1943), p. 85.

Several Benedictions Found in Scripture

The architecture of Hebrews is like a grand cathedral. Its themes are lofty. Its arching revelation about the supremacy of Christ is awe-inspiring. Its alcoves of Old Testament allusions are unparalleled in the New Testament. And like any worship service held in a cathedral, it draws to a close with a benediction.

In a High Church setting, the invocation calls for the blessing of God at the onset of the worship service. The benediction, however, calls for God's blessing on the parishioners at the end of the service.

Benedictions are found throughout the Old and New Testaments. Several stand out in particular.

Numbers 6:24–26

Through Moses God told Aaron and his sons to bless the children of Israel, in one of the most heartwarming passages in all of Scripture.

> "'The Lord bless you, and keep you;
> The Lord make His face shine on you,
> And be gracious to you;
> The Lord lift up His countenance on you,
> And give you peace.'"

2 Corinthians 13:14

Paul closes his second letter to the Corinthians with these words of blessing:

> The grace of the Lord Jesus Christ, and the love of God, and the fellowship of the Holy Spirit, be with you all.

Jude 24–25

Jude closes his brief letter with a doxology of praise for the many blessings of God.

> Now to Him who is able to keep you from stumbling, and to make you stand in the presence of His glory blameless with great joy, to the only God our Savior, through Jesus Christ our Lord, be glory, majesty, dominion and authority, before all time and now and forever. Amen.

A Specific Benediction regarding God's Will

As the writer to the Hebrews jots down his closing remarks, he pauses pensively, then dips his pen in the inkwell to inscribe this very personal doxology of delight:

> Now the God of peace, who brought up from the dead the great Shepherd of the sheep through the blood of the eternal covenant, even Jesus our Lord, equip you in every good thing to do His will, working in us that which is pleasing in His sight, through Jesus Christ, to whom be the glory forever and ever. Amen. (13:20–21)

Remember the recipients of that letter when you read the benediction. They were Christians who had been taken by the scruff of the neck and booted down the back steps of the community. They were out on the street, left to the alleyways to forage for some scant leftover of hope.

As they pored over the fragments of their shattered lives, they must have wrestled with the will of God. They must have wondered where God was and why He seemed so silent.

It is on such disheartened ears that the writer's benediction falls. It talks about God's will and tells us three important facts about it.

Who Makes God's Will Happen?

Verse 20 refers to the Almighty as "the God of *peace*" (emphasis added). A practical paraphrase of this term might be "mental health," for God desires there to be a calm within our hearts, not panic. He wants there to be an inner assurance that He is in control (see Ps. 46 and John 14:1–3).

The meaning of the word *peace* is crucial not only to understanding the nature of God but also to understanding the outworking of His will on earth. Listen to what one writer says about its Hebrew translation, *shalom.*

> *Shālôm* means "absence of strife" in approximately fifty to sixty usages: e.g. I Kgs 4:25 . . . reflects the safety of the nation in the peaceful days of Solomon when the land and its neighbors had been subdued.
>
> "Peace," in this case, means much more than the mere absence of war. Rather, the root meaning of the verb *shālēm* better expresses the true concept of *shālôm.* Completeness, wholeness, harmony, fulfillment, are closer to the meaning. Implicit in *shālôm* is the idea

> of unimpaired relationships with others and fulfillment in one's undertakings.[2]

This type of peace is not something the world offers; it is divine in origin, sourced in the very nature of God (see John 14:27).

The classic statement of this concept of peace is found in the benediction we read from Numbers 6:24–26: ". . . The Lord lift up His countenance on you, And give you *peace*" (emphasis added).

The next phrase in Hebrews 13:20—"who brought up from the dead the great Shepherd of the sheep"—shows that our God is not only a God of peace, He's also a God of power. His power raised Jesus from the dead. And if He can give new life to the dead, He can resurrect any hope—no matter how lifeless, how stiff, or how cold.

Generally, when we think of power, we think of military might. We think of nuclear arms and combat troops. But God's power is different. His is a power that exudes from brokenness, a power that shines light out of darkness, a power that brings life out of death.

The United Nations is a monument to man's never-ending quest for peace. In fact, the U.N. building bears the chiseled words of Isaiah 2:4—"They shall beat their swords into plowshares, and their spears into pruninghooks: nation shall not lift up sword against nation, neither shall they learn war any more."

But just as the U.N. is a monument to man's search for peace, it is also a monument to man's impotence in attaining any real or lasting peace on earth. Why? Because true peace is found not in the eloquently crafted lines of a nation's constitution. Because it doesn't reside in the heart of man. It springs only from Jesus Christ.

He is the Prince of Peace, and until every knee bows in recognition of that fact, there will not be peace on earth or good will toward men.

How Does God's Will Happen?

In Hebrews 13:20 the writer refers to Jesus as "the great Shepherd of the sheep," an image Christ used of Himself in John 10:11. Because He is our Shepherd we have no need for concern—we "shall not want" (Ps. 23:1). He will nourish and refresh us (vv. 2–3). And He will protect us from the wolves that would attack us (compare v. 5 with John 10:11–15).

2. G. Lloyd Carr, "*Shālēm,*" *Theological Wordbook of the Old Testament,* ed. R. Laird Harris, Gleason L. Archer, Jr., and Bruce K. Waltke (Chicago, Ill.: Moody Press, 1980), vol. 2, p. 931.

As sheep, we are prone to wander, as Isaiah 53:6a tells us—"All of us like sheep have gone astray, / Each of us has turned to his own way." Fortunately, however, our Shepherd knows that. He personally guides us in the paths of righteousness (Ps. 23:3).

As sheep, we are also defenseless. Sheep do not have sharp teeth or swift legs or straight horns with which to do battle. How then does our Shepherd protect us? The answer is found in Hebrews 13:21—He *equips* us "in every good thing to do His will."

The term *equip* carries with it the idea of "restoring, helping along, giving encouraging thoughts." The writer to the Hebrews expresses in his benediction the idea that God is fighting for us in our corner of the ring, not fighting against us or sitting passively in the stands (see Rom. 8:31–39). Leon Morris articulates the meaning of the term in the context of Hebrews.

> The verb "equip" (*katartizō*) is often used of mending what is broken and torn, and some see a reference to putting right what was amiss in the spiritual life of the readers. A prayer that God would put things right would be quite in place. But in this context perhaps the meaning is "supply you with what you need to live the Christian life."[3]

Not only does the Lord equip us, but He works in us to do His will—a fact corroborated by Philippians 2:13.

> For it is God who is at work in you, both to will and to work for His good pleasure.

It's important to understand where the ultimate responsibility rests—with God. We are not working *for* Him; He is working *in* us (see 2 Cor. 3:5, 4:7).

We are like passengers on a 747 jet. The way we travel is to rest in Him. His power is what will get us to our destination, not the frenzied flapping of our own wings.

The Result That Follows

The latter part of Hebrews 13:21 reveals the results of His equipping and working in us. When we do His will, we bring Him glory, which is why we were put on this earth to begin with (see 1 Cor. 10:31).

3. Leon Morris, "Hebrews," *The Expositor's Bible Commentary,* gen. ed. Frank E. Gaebelein (Grand Rapids, Mich.: Zondervan Publishing House, Regency Reference Library, 1981), vol. 12, p. 155.

Some Concluding Thoughts

As we approach the close of this study, let's come full circle and return to the benediction of Hebrews 13:20–21.

> Now the God of peace, who brought up from the dead the great Shepherd of the sheep through the blood of the eternal covenant, even Jesus our Lord, equip you in every good thing to do His will, working in us that which is pleasing in His sight, through Jesus Christ, to whom be the glory forever and ever. Amen.

Reflect on those two verses, won't you? They should sink deeply within our hearts and affect us in three areas regarding God, His will, and His glory.

Regarding God: Since He is a God of peace who cannot die, we should stop worrying (see 1 Cor. 15:12–28). Regarding His will: Since we cannot fulfill His will on our own, we should stop trying to manufacture fruit. We should simply abide in the Vine and allow His power to be manifested in our lives (see John 15:1–5). Regarding His glory: Since God's glory cannot be shared, we should stop striving for it (see Isa. 48:11, Ps. 46:10a).

Shalom!

Living Insights — STUDY ONE

This study included an overview of some of the benedictions found in the Bible. These verses are often read through quickly, but today let's examine them at an unhurried pace.

- Look up each of the following benedictions and read them carefully. Look specifically for doctrinal truths that you'd like to remember. As you finish, take a little time to savor the richness of these passages.

Benedictions

Numbers 6:24–26

2 Corinthians 13:14

____

____

____

____

1 Thessalonians 5:23

____

____

____

____

Jude 24, 25

____

____

____

____

Living Insights STUDY TWO

We learned an important truth from Hebrews 13:21—when we do God's will, our actions bring Him glory. Is this apparent in your life? Let's look at the two main aspects of this point.

- God's Will

1. Do you feel you are in God's will? ____________________

____

____

2. Why or why not? ____________________________

____

____

3. What one thing could you be doing to be more in God's will?

____

____

____

____

- Glorifying God

1. What does this phrase mean? ______________________________

____

____

2. How can you know when you're glorifying God or not?

____

____

____

____

3. What is easy about it? What's difficult? ______________________________

____

____

____

Chapter 20

An Urgent Farewell

Hebrews 13:22–25

In Tennyson's *Idylls of the King,* King Arthur is on his deathbed as his funeral barge prepares to push out to sea. In a heartrending scene, the dying king bids an urgent farewell to his loyal friend Sir Bedivere.

> 'If thou shouldst never see my face again,
> Pray for my soul. More things are wrought by prayer
> Than this world dreams of. Wherefore, let thy voice
> Rise like a fountain for me night and day.
> For what are men better than sheep or goats
> That nourish a blind life within the brain,
> If, knowing God, they lift not hands of prayer
> Both for themselves and those who call them friend?
> For so the whole round earth is every way
> Bound by gold chains about the feet of God.
> But now farewell. I am going a long way
> With these thou seëst—if indeed I go
> (For all my mind is clouded with a doubt)—
> To the island-valley of Avilion;
> Where falls not hail, or rain, or any snow.
> Nor ever wind blows loudly; but it lies
> Deep-meadow'd, happy, fair with orchard lawns
> And bowery hollows crown'd with summer sea,
> Where I will heal me of my grievous wound.'[1]

As in the closing of a life, the closing of a letter often includes an urgent farewell. The letter to the Hebrews is no exception.

There we will see the heart of the writer revealed in all its warmth and loving concern. And there we will stand on the shore to say good-bye to our good friend who has so stirred our hearts.

A Review of the Warnings

Before we bid our final farewell, it might be helpful to reminisce about the passages that have changed our lives. Probably topping

1. Alfred, Lord Tennyson, "The Passing of Arthur," *Idylls of the King,* ed. Willis Boughton (Boston, Mass.: Ginn and Co., 1913), pp. 155–56.

that list would be the sobering warnings woven throughout the fabric of the letter. The writer urgently warns us to:

1. Guard against drifting and neglecting (2:1–4).
2. Stay sensitive and be alert (3:12–14).
3. Grow up (5:11–14).
4. Reject carnality (10:26–31).
5. Heed the Word (12:25–29).

Three Urgent Commands

Let's change gears now and downshift our attention from the five urgent warnings to three urgent commands.

Bear with the Truth of God

The writer's first concern is stated in 13:22.

> But I urge you, brethren, bear with this word of exhortation, for I have written to you briefly.

To get a glimpse of the writer's deeper meaning, we need to understand a couple of key words and phrases. The first key word, *urge,* is from the Greek term *parakaleō,* which

> seems to mean something more like "I beg you." . . . There is appeal in it, but also encouragement. The letter has had its share of rebukes and stern warnings, and the writer now softens the impact a little with this appeal and with the affectionate address "Brothers."[2]

From this word alone we can see that the desire of this writer's heart is that his readers do more than merely nod their assent to the truths he has so painstakingly presented to them. He doesn't want them shelving away the notes they've been taking. He wants them to *bear with* the teaching. This is the next key phrase, which literally means "to listen to, hold up, endure."

The process of "bearing with" begins by hearing (compare Rom. 10:17 with James 1:19). Hearing gives the seeds of truth the opportunity to sink in and take root. But hearing is only the first stage in the process. The goal is bearing fruit. Think of the parable of the

2. Leon Morris, "Hebrews," *The Expositor's Bible Commentary,* gen. ed. Frank E. Gaebelein (Grand Rapids, Mich.: Zondervan Publishing House, Regency Reference Library, 1981), vol. 12, p. 156.

soils, and you'll get a pretty good visual aid of what the writer is looking for in the lives of his readers (see Matt. 13:1–8, 18–23).

In the writer's urging his readers to apply what they've heard, there is an application for us as well. How easy it is for us to stuff our mental shelves with notebooks full of biblical truth. How easy it is to live the cerebral Christian life instead of the committed Christian life. Perhaps that is the single most common ailment in the body of Christ—trafficking in unlived truth—which explains why hypocrisy runs so rampant.

Listen to the words of another New Testament writer, who not only shows us what "bear with" means but also gives us an antidote for hypocrisy.

> Do not neglect the spiritual gift within you, which was bestowed upon you through prophetic utterance with the laying on of hands by the presbytery. Take pains with these things; be absorbed in them, so that your progress may be evident to all. Pay close attention to yourself and to your teaching; persevere in these things; for as you do this you will insure salvation both for yourself and for those who hear you. (1 Tim. 4:14–16)

Now that we've examined this first command in the closing comments of Hebrews, let's turn to the second.

Take Notice of the People of God

In Hebrews 13:23 the writer changes focus from the truth of God to the people of God.

> Take notice that our brother Timothy has been released, with whom, if he comes soon, I shall see you.

This comment refers to Paul's close friend and fellow laborer in the ministry, Timothy, whose "release" most likely refers to being let out of prison. This would then prepare the way for Timothy to accompany the writer to visit the Hebrews in person.[3]

By way of application, we should "take notice" of believers who are in prison and pray for their release—whether that prison be the actual bars of a jail cell or some psychological or emotional bars

3. "The verb [*release*] has a wide range of meaning. It is used, for example, of releasing Paul and Barnabas for missionary work (Acts 13:3; cf. 15:30, 33), but its most frequent sense in the New Testament is that of releasing from custody persons who are under arrest or in prison." Philip Edgcumbe Hughes, *A Commentary on the Epistle to the Hebrews* (Grand Rapids, Mich.: William B. Eerdmans Publishing Co., 1977), p. 593.

that keep them from being free (see Acts 12:1–10, Heb. 13:3, Prov. 18:19).

How sensitive are your spiritual antennae in feeling out the needs of others? If the person has recently been released from some difficulty and needs your friendship, are you available and willing to be involved? Remember how Barnabas got involved with Christianity's Public Enemy Number One, who had just been converted on the Damascus road (Acts 9:26–27).

Express and Accept Greetings

The final command issued by the writer to the Hebrews is found in 13:24.

> Greet all of your leaders and all the saints. Those from Italy greet you.

This verse begins with an imperative—*greet*—and ends in an indicative—"those from Italy *greet* you" (emphasis added). The emphasis is on the free-flowing nature of Christian hospitality. When you read through the New Testament, you realize how affectionate and embracing the early Christians were. Not only did they touch each other, they kissed each other as well (see Acts 20:37, Rom. 16:16, 1 Pet. 5:14).

For some reason, twentieth-century Christianity has become a cool, detached, touch-me-not religion. And yet touch is fundamental not only to our psychological welfare but our physical health as well.[4]

It is important that when we tighten our shoes and our ties on Sunday morning, we don't tighten our personalities in the process. Because relational charley horses serve no purpose in the body of Christ—except to inflict pain and cripple it.

Grace: A Final Farewell

Realizing that he and Timothy might be hindered in coming to them, the writer leaves his readers with a final word of farewell. That word is not "Obey my warnings, or else!" or "Behave yourselves!" Nor is it "Live and let live!" or "Enjoy yourselves!"

That word is *grace*—"Grace be with you all" (Heb. 13:25).

4. For further study on this subject consult Gary Smalley and John Trent's excellent book *The Blessing* (Nashville, Tenn.: Thomas Nelson Publishers, 1986)—especially the chapter "The First Element of Blessing: Meaningful Touch." See also Luke 7:36–50 for a biblical example praised by the Savior.

The final short benediction, identical with that of Titus 3:15 (cf. 2 Tim. 4:22), is a prayer that *grace* . . . may be with them all. This grace, says Spicq, "is a stream of living water flowing through the desert, a power which enables us to withstand every adversity and to reach the promised land, the place of our rest, the heavenly Jerusalem."[5]

Hebrews in Review: Some Practical Conclusions

The letter to the Hebrews may be a beautifully woven piece of theology, but if we leave it on a hanger in our mental closet, it does us no practical good. We not only have to take off our stiff, old preconceptions about Christianity, we have to put on the resplendent truths that have been so painstakingly tailored to clothe us.

Let's try three of those truths on for size. And remember as you're staring in the full-length mirror—it's not so important for us to go through Hebrews as it is for Hebrews to go through us.

Theme: The Superiority of Christ

For Hebrews to go through us, Christ must become superior within us. We must model His acceptance of others, His sensitive walk with God, and His power to handle circumstances (see Matt. 10:25a, Phil. 2:3–8, 1 Pet. 2:21–23).

Message: The Practicality of Christianity

For Hebrews to go through us, our faith must move from the theoretical realm to the practical. It must affect our prayer life, our attitudes, our relationships. It must change us—not simply inform us (see Gal. 5:16–25, Eph. 4:17–32).

Goal: The Maturity of Christians

For Hebrews to go through us, our lives must be marked with liberty rather than rigidity. That is the hallmark of maturity (see John 8:32, Rom. 8:15, 2 Cor. 3:17, Gal. 5:1).

Living Insights STUDY ONE

The letter to the Hebrews was one of encouragement to those whose faith was being challenged by the rising waters of persecution and the gale-force winds of disillusionment. What they needed was

5. Hughes, *A Commentary on the Epistle to the Hebrews*, p. 594.

something solid to hold on to, something to steady them through the storm. That is why the writer placed such emphasis on the person and work of Christ. He is our bridge over troubled waters. He is our friend when friends just can't be found. He is our light when darkness falls so hard and pain is all around.

Do you have a friend who's going through some stormy times right now? Write that person a letter of encouragement, won't you? And for that friend who is weary and feeling small, you might want to postscript your letter with the affirming words of Isaiah 40:29–31.

> He gives strength to the weary,
> And to him who lacks might He increases power.
> Though youths grow weary and tired,
> And vigorous young men stumble badly,
> Yet those who wait for the Lord
> Will gain new strength;
> They will mount up with wings like eagles,
> They will run and not get tired,
> They will walk and not become weary.

Living Insights STUDY TWO

As we conclude our time in Hebrews, there is a key question each of us must ask: How much of Hebrews has penetrated my life?

- Let's review the studies we've done together. Look back through your notes and focus on the most significant biblical truth you discovered in each message. Then look for a specific area of application that touched your life in each particular study.

The Practical Life of Faith

How to Cure the Shrinks

Truth ____

____

____

Application ____

____

____

Common Men of Uncommon Faith

Truth ____

____

____

Application ____

____

____

A Faith Worth Duplicating

Truth ____

____

____

Application ____

____

____

The Ultimate Test

Truth ____

____

____

Application ____

____

____

Faith Served Family Style

Truth ____

____

____

Application ____

____

____

Moses' Faith, Moses' Choices . . . and Me

Truth ____

____

____

Application ____

____

____

By Faith, Miracles!

Truth ____

____

____

Application ____

____

____

Triumphs and Tragedies of the Faithful

Truth ____

____

____

Application ____

____

____

Arena Lifestyle

Truth ____

____

____

Application ____

____

____

Flip Side of Love

Truth ______________________________

____

____

Application ______________________________

____

____

Watch Out for Worldliness!

Truth ______________________________

____

____

Application ______________________________

____

____

Our Awesome, Consuming God

Truth ______________________________

____

____

Application ______________________________

____

____

Brothers, Strangers, and Prisoners

Truth ______________________________

____

____

Application ______________________________

____

____

Commitment and Contentment (Part One)

Truth ____

____

____

Application ____

____

____

Commitment and Contentment (Part Two)

Truth ____

____

____

Application ____

____

____

My Responsibility to God-Appointed Leaders

Truth ____

____

____

Application ____

____

____

Changeless Truths in a Shiftless World

Truth ____

____

____

Application ____

____

____

Daring the Risk of Reach

Truth ____

____

____

Application ____

____

____

Equipped to Do His Will

Truth ____

____

____

Application ____

____

____

An Urgent Farewell

Truth ____

____

____

Application ____

____

____

Books for Probing Further

Hebrews 11 is commonly referred to as *The Hall of Faith.* Framed within that gallery are paragraph portraits of those who exemplified lives of faith. There are no picture-perfect saints in the collection; every one has some flaw visible for all the world to see, and those flaws are brushed with lifelike strokes in the rest of Scripture.

In this portion of the Bible, however, the forgiving lighting of God's grace shines on these portraits in such a way as to highlight the beauty of their faith while hiding the blemishes.

If we wanted to turn up the lights, we'd find that Noah got drunk, Abraham lied, Sarah laughed at the revelation of God, Jacob was a manipulator, Moses committed manslaughter, Samson was a fornicator, David was an adulterer and a murderer. So we're not talking about photogenic models with every ethical hair in place. We're talking about ordinary people—but people who believed in God in an extraordinary way.

Hebrews 11 is the one chapter of the Bible that could continue to be written. Every generation, ordinary people rise up to believe God in extraordinary ways. Flawed people. Irregular people. People like us.

Some of their flaws are theological. Some of their irregularities are moral ones. But their lives are murals that exhibit dramatic profiles of faith.

To further your study of Hebrews, we thought you'd enjoy reading about the lives of a few of these giants in the faith. A handful of important resources are listed below.

Eareckson, Joni, with Joe Musser. *Joni.* Grand Rapids, Mich.: Zondervan Publishing House, 1976. The true story of a young woman's permanently paralyzing diving accident, this moving account brings the reader into the depths of her despair as well as the heights of her triumphant faith. It is an inspiration and encouragement to all who have had to trust God when the bottom has dropped out of their life.

Foxe, John. *Foxe's Book of Martyrs.* Prepared by W. Grinton Berry. Reprint. Grand Rapids, Mich.: Baker Book House, 1987. Written in the mid-1500s, this remarkable classic chronicles the lives, sufferings, and triumphant deaths of Christian martyrs throughout history. Beginning with the first martyr, Jesus Christ, Foxe traces the persecution of the church throughout the centuries.

Muggeridge, Malcolm. *Something Beautiful for God.* San Francisco, Calif.: Harper and Row, Publishers, 1971. This renowned theologian writes about Mother Teresa of Calcutta, one of the most stirring examples of Christian love in our lifetime. He paints a profoundly moving portrait by giving an overview of her work, a collection of her sayings, and a personal interview.

Robertson, Edwin. *The Shame and the Sacrifice.* New York, N.Y.: Macmillan Publishing Co., 1988. This is a biography of Dietrich Bonhoeffer, a German-Lutheran pastor who met with martyrdom at the hands of the Nazis. His days in the Gestapo prisons were full of faith and loyal ministry for the Savior.

Sayer, George. *Jack: C. S. Lewis and His Times.* San Francisco, Calif.: Harper and Row, Publishers, 1988. Longtime friend and colleague of C. S. Lewis, the author writes from the perspective of a trusted member of Lewis' inner circle. Lewis was one of the greatest and most original apologists for the Christian faith, and his books still inspire millions.

ten Boom, Corrie, with John and Elizabeth Sherrill. *The Hiding Place.* Old Tappan, N.J.: Fleming H. Revell Co., 1971. This book tells of the incredible courage of a Christian family who smuggled Jews to freedom but were unable to escape the Nazi concentration camps themselves. It is a story of incredible faith.

Tucker, Ruth A. *Sacred Stories: Daily Devotions from the Family of God.* Grand Rapids, Mich.: Zondervan Publishing House, Daybreak Books, 1989. This book is a collection of historical and contemporary testimonies of Christians from around the world. Its format is anecdotal, and it tells compelling, one-page stories about the faithful, from Martin Luther to Corrie ten Boom.

Woodbridge, John D., gen. ed. *Great Leaders of the Christian Church.* Chicago, Ill.: Moody Press, 1988. This book offers thumbnail sketches of heroes of the faith, ranging from the apostle Paul to Francis Schaeffer. Each article gives a brief chronology of the person's life, the person's place in church history, and a biographical profile.

Wurmbrand, Richard. *Tortured for Christ.* Westchester, Ill.: Good News Publishers, Crossway Books, 1987. The author recounts the courage and faith of believers behind the Iron Curtain and shows that the persecution of the church is not something indigenous to first-century Christians alone.

NOTES

NOTES

Notes

NOTES

Insight for Living
Cassette Tapes
THE PRACTICAL LIFE OF FAITH

The first ten chapters of Hebrews established Christ's preeminence. But once we grasp this truth, how should we respond? "Walk by faith" is the challenge in the concluding chapters of this New Testament letter. Here we're reminded of those whose lives were characterized by a living faith—from Abel to Abraham, from Moses to the martyrs. And with our eyes on Christ, we're encouraged to live as they lived . . . by faith.

			U.S.	Canada
PLF	CS	**Cassette series—includes album cover . .**	**$55.25**	$70.00
		Individual cassettes—include messages A and B	**5.00**	6.35

These prices are subject to change without notice.

PLF 1-A: ***How to Cure the Shrinks***—Hebrews 10:32–11:6
B: ***Common Men of Uncommon Faith***—Hebrews 11:1–7

PLF 2-A: ***A Faith Worth Duplicating***—Hebrews 11:8–16
B: ***The Ultimate Test***—Hebrews 11:17–19, Genesis 22

PLF 3-A: ***Faith Served Family Style***—Hebrews 11:20–23
B: ***Moses' Faith, Moses' Choices . . . and Me***—Hebrews 11:24–28

PLF 4-A: ***By Faith, Miracles!***—Hebrews 11:29–31
B: ***Triumphs and Tragedies of the Faithful***—Hebrews 11:32–40

PLF 5-A: ***Arena Lifestyle***—Hebrews 12:1–3
B: ***Flip Side of Love***—Hebrews 12:4–13

PLF 6-A: ***Watch Out for Worldliness!***—Hebrews 12:14–17
B: ***Our Awesome, Consuming God***—Hebrews 12:18–29

PLF 7-A: ***Brothers, Strangers, and Prisoners***—Hebrews 13:1–3
B: ***Commitment and Contentment (Part One)***—Hebrews 13:4

PLF 8-A: ***Commitment and Contentment (Part Two)***—Hebrews 13:5–6
B: ***My Responsibility to God-Appointed Leaders***—Hebrews 13:7, 17; Matthew 15:1–14

PLF 9-A: ***Changeless Truths in a Shiftless World***—Hebrews 13:8–16
B: ***Daring the Risk of Reach***—Hebrews 13:18–19, Ephesians 6:11–20, Mark 9:17–29

PLF 10-A: ***Equipped to Do His Will***—Hebrews 13:20–21
B: ***An Urgent Farewell***—Hebrews 13:22–25

How to Order by Mail

Simply mark on the order form whether you want the series or individual tapes. Mail the form with your payment to the appropriate address listed below. We will process your order as promptly as we can.

United States: Mail your order to the Sales Department at Insight for Living, Post Office Box 4444, Fullerton, California 92634. If you wish your order to be shipped first-class for faster delivery, add 10 percent of the total order amount (not including California sales tax). Otherwise, please allow four to six weeks for delivery by fourth-class mail. We accept personal checks, money orders, Visa, or MasterCard in payment for materials. Unfortunately, we are unable to offer invoicing or COD orders.

Canada: Mail your order to Insight for Living Ministries, Post Office Box 2510, Vancouver, British Columbia V6B 3W7. Please add 7 percent of your total order for first-class postage and allow approximately four weeks for delivery. Our listeners in British Columbia must also add a 6 percent sales tax to the total of all tape orders (not including postage). We accept personal checks, money orders, Visa, or MasterCard in payment for materials. Unfortunately, we are unable to offer invoicing or COD orders.

Australia, New Zealand, or Papua New Guinea: Mail your order to Insight for Living, Inc., GPO Box 2823 EE, Melbourne, Victoria 3001, Australia. Please allow six to ten weeks for delivery by surface mail. If you would like your order sent airmail, the delivery time may be reduced. Whether you choose surface or airmail, postage costs must be added to the amount of purchase and included with your order. Please use the chart that follows to determine correct postage. Due to fluctuating currency rates, we can accept only personal checks made payable in U.S. funds, international money orders, Visa, or MasterCard in payment for materials.

Overseas: Other overseas residents should contact our United States office. Please allow six to ten weeks for delivery by surface mail. If you would like your order sent airmail, the delivery time may be reduced. Whether you choose surface or airmail, postage costs must be added to the amount of purchase and included with your order. Please use the chart that follows to determine correct postage. Due to fluctuating currency rates, we can accept only personal checks made payable in U.S. funds, international money orders, Visa, or MasterCard in payment for materials.

Type of Postage	Postage Cost
Surface	10% of total order
Airmail	25% of total order

For Faster Service, Order by Telephone

To purchase using Visa or MasterCard, you are welcome to use our **toll-free** numbers between the hours of 8:30 A.M. and 4:00 P.M., Pacific time, Monday through Friday. The number to call from anywhere in the United States is **1-800-772-8888.** To order from Canada, call our Vancouver office at **1-800-663-7639.** Vancouver residents should call (604) 272-5811. Telephone orders from overseas are handled through our Sales Department at (714) 870-9161. We are unable to accept collect calls.

Our Guarantee

Our cassettes are guaranteed for ninety days against faulty performance or breakage due to a defect in the tape. For best results, please be sure your tape recorder is in good operating condition and is cleaned regularly.

Note: To cover processing and handling, there is a $10 fee for *any* returned check.

Order Form

PLF CS represents the entire *The Practical Life of Faith* series, while PLF 1–10 are the individual tapes included in the series.

Series or Tape	Unit Price U.S.	Unit Price Canada	Quantity	Amount
PLF CS	$55.25	$70.00		$
PLF 1	5.00	6.35		
PLF 2	5.00	6.35		
PLF 3	5.00	6.35		
PLF 4	5.00	6.35		
PLF 5	5.00	6.35		
PLF 6	5.00	6.35		
PLF 7	5.00	6.35		
PLF 8	5.00	6.35		
PLF 9	5.00	6.35		
PLF 10	5.00	6.35		
Subtotal				
Sales tax *6¼% for orders delivered in California; 6% in British Columbia*				
Postage *7% in Canada; overseas residents, see "How to Order by Mail"*				
10% optional first-class shipping and handling *United States residents only*				
Gift to Insight for Living *Tax-deductible in the United States and Canada*				
Total amount due *Please do not send cash.*				$

If there is a balance: ☐ apply it as a donation ☐ please refund

Form of payment:

☐ Check or money order made payable to Insight for Living

☐ Credit card (circle one): Visa MasterCard

Card Number ____________________ Expiration Date __________

Signature ________________________________

We cannot process your credit card purchase without your signature.

Name ________________________________

Address ________________________________

City ____________________ State/Province __________

Zip/Postal Code ______________ Country ______________

Telephone ( ) ______________ Radio Station ___ ___ ___ ___

If questions arise concerning your order, we may need to contact you.

Mail this order form to the Sales Department at one of these addresses:

Insight for Living, Post Office Box 4444, Fullerton, CA 92634

Insight for Living Ministries, Post Office Box 2510, Vancouver, BC, Canada V6B 3W7

Insight for Living, Inc., GPO Box 2823 EE, Melbourne, VIC 3001, Australia

Order Form

PLF CS represents the entire *The Practical Life of Faith* series, while PLF 1–10 are the individual tapes included in the series.

Series or Tape	Unit Price U.S.	Unit Price Canada	Quantity	Amount
PLF CS	$55.25	$70.00		$
PLF 1	5.00	6.35		
PLF 2	5.00	6.35		
PLF 3	5.00	6.35		
PLF 4	5.00	6.35		
PLF 5	5.00	6.35		
PLF 6	5.00	6.35		
PLF 7	5.00	6.35		
PLF 8	5.00	6.35		
PLF 9	5.00	6.35		
PLF 10	5.00	6.35		
Subtotal				
Sales tax *6¼% for orders delivered in California; 6% in British Columbia*				
Postage *7% in Canada; overseas residents, see "How to Order by Mail"*				
10% optional first-class shipping and handling *United States residents only*				
Gift to Insight for Living *Tax-deductible in the United States and Canada*				
Total amount due *Please do not send cash.*				$

If there is a balance: ☐ apply it as a donation ☐ please refund

Form of payment:

☐ Check or money order made payable to Insight for Living

☐ Credit card (circle one): Visa MasterCard

Card Number ____________ Expiration Date ____________

Signature ________________________

We cannot process your credit card purchase without your signature.

Name ________________________

Address ________________________

City ____________ State/Province ____________

Zip/Postal Code ____________ Country ____________

Telephone ( ) ____________ Radio Station ____________

If questions arise concerning your order, we may need to contact you.

Mail this order form to the Sales Department at one of these addresses:

Insight for Living, Post Office Box 4444, Fullerton, CA 92634

Insight for Living Ministries, Post Office Box 2510, Vancouver, BC, Canada V6B 3W7

Insight for Living, Inc., GPO Box 2823 EE, Melbourne, VIC 3001, Australia

Order Form

PLF CS represents the entire *The Practical Life of Faith* series, while PLF 1–10 are the individual tapes included in the series.

Series or Tape	Unit Price U.S.	Unit Price Canada	Quantity	Amount
PLF CS	$55.25	$70.00		$
PLF 1	5.00	6.35		
PLF 2	5.00	6.35		
PLF 3	5.00	6.35		
PLF 4	5.00	6.35		
PLF 5	5.00	6.35		
PLF 6	5.00	6.35		
PLF 7	5.00	6.35		
PLF 8	5.00	6.35		
PLF 9	5.00	6.35		
PLF 10	5.00	6.35		
Subtotal				
Sales tax *6¼% for orders delivered in California; 6% in British Columbia*				
Postage *7% in Canada; overseas residents, see "How to Order by Mail"*				
10% optional first-class shipping and handling *United States residents only*				
Gift to Insight for Living *Tax-deductible in the United States and Canada*				
Total amount due *Please do not send cash.*				$

If there is a balance: ☐ apply it as a donation ☐ please refund

Form of payment:

☐ Check or money order made payable to Insight for Living

☐ Credit card (circle one): Visa MasterCard

Card Number ______________________ Expiration Date ___________

Signature ____

We cannot process your credit card purchase without your signature.

Name ____

Address ____

City ______________________ State/Province___________

Zip/Postal Code ______________ Country ______________

Telephone (   ) ______________ Radio Station ___ ___ ___ ___

If questions arise concerning your order, we may need to contact you.

Mail this order form to the Sales Department at one of these addresses:

Insight for Living, Post Office Box 4444, Fullerton, CA 92634

Insight for Living Ministries, Post Office Box 2510, Vancouver, BC, Canada V6B 3W7

Insight for Living, Inc., GPO Box 2823 EE, Melbourne, VIC 3001, Australia